D0119512

BREAKFAST IN BRIGHTON

BREAKFAST IN BRIGHTON

Adventures on the Edge of Britain

Nigel Richardson

VICTOR GOLLANCZ

LONDON

First published in Great Britain 1998
by Victor Gollancz
An imprint of the Cassell Group
Wellington House, 125 Strand, London WC2R 0BB

© Nigel Richardson 1998

The right of Nigel Richardson to be identified as author of
this work has been asserted by him in accordance with
the Copyright, Designs and Patents Act, 1988.

A catalogue record for this book is
available from the British Library.

ISBN 0 575 06600 8

Typeset by Rowland Phototypesetting Ltd
Bury St Edmunds, Suffolk
Printed in Great Britain by
St Edmundsbury Press Ltd, Bury St Edmunds, Suffolk

98 99 5 4 3 2

While Brighton slept – North Street, West Street, East Street, Western Road, Preston Street, Hove, the hotels, the shops, the restaurants, the movies, the baths, the booths, the churches, the Market, the Post Office, the pubs, the antiques, the second-hand books – slept and gleamed and climbed up from the sea under the dark blue dawn, the enormous gloomy man walked along the front, hardly visible in the darkness, seemingly the only wayfarer, the only one awake. And he looked out at the sea and wondered what it was he had to do.

Patrick Hamilton, *Hangover Square*

Acknowledgements

The author makes grateful acknowledgements to the following for permission to use copyright material in this book: Constable Publishers for the extract from *Hangover Square* by Patrick Hamilton; Heinemann and The Bodley Head for extracts from Graham Greene's *Brighton Rock* and *Ways of Escape* respectively; Mark Hamilton as the Literary Executor of the Estate of the late Sonia Brownell Orwell, and Martin Secker & Warburg and AM Heath & Co Ltd, for the extract from 'Decline of the English Murder' by George Orwell; to Harold Pinter and Faber & Faber Ltd for the extract from 'A Note on Shakespeare' from *Various Voices*. The extract from *The Waste Land*, from *Collected Poems 1909–1962* by T. S. Elliot, appears by permission of Faber & Faber Ltd.

I am indebted to the following in the writing of this book: Peter and Donald and the crew in the Grosvenor; Maire McQueeney; Mike Strong; Fredda Hayworth; Brian Behan; Graham; Francis Carr; Carol Marsh; Roy Boulting; Mary Welford; Jack and Wayne; James Warren; Jennifer Pearse; Paddy and Robin Burt; Paul Cemmick; James Morrison; Byron Rogers; Alex Hamilton; Flo; Queenspark Books; Paul Mansfield; Frank Windsor.

Extra special thanks to: Paul Spencer and Nicky Smith, whose lives I borrowed; Roger Tollervey, who lit a piece of paper; Gill Charlton, for the time and much else; Mike Petty, who got it straight away; and of course, and as ever, Miren.

Chapter One

Meeting Fredda was a major stroke of luck. She lived near the Grosvenor Arms in Brunswick Terrace, one of the grandest Regency terraces in Brighton and Hove, one of the finest petals in that seafront flowering of Venetian vistas that happened in the 1820s. Normally Fredda would rent rooms only to actors but she made an exception for me. Within a few days I had moved my things into a room in the attic of the house, at the front, with three small, shuttered sash windows looking out over the beach and sea – if I raise my head from my keyboard, I can just see the horizon, the point where the sea meets the sky, beautifully silver where the sun is bursting through the clouds.

Fredda's house, and the Regency development of which it is part, was where the fabric and spirit of Brighton achieved dazzling harmony. In the eighteenth century Brighton was still a fishing hamlet with snub nose, freckles and an awkward name: Brighthelmstone. One night the seagulls went to sleep and when they woke up their little town was cool and knowing, ingeniously sexy. Norma Jean Baker became Marilyn Monroe. It was one of history's great makeovers. Getting pissed in the Grosvenor, I had stumbled into the heart of the place.

The Grosvenor Arms was good at that. It was the size and shape of the pub, but more than its size and shape, which drew people together. The Grosvenor was small and looked screamingly dainty from the outside, with its white façade decorated with pale blue raised plasterwork and a bay window of frosted lights which glowed orange from 11 a.m. onwards. You measured it in your mind's eye as you crossed Little Western Street towards it and if you hadn't been feeling crapulent – in other words, if you hadn't been in the Grosvenor the night before – you would have fancied your chances of leaping and touching the window-ledges of the first floor, it was that compact.

The door was open in licensing hours, exhaling gusts of laughter and hops, Roy Orbison and barking dogs, on to the windy little street that ran down to the sea. Affixed to the ceiling at the back end of the bar, in full view from outside, was a single red spotlight. This functioned as a stage light on the few occasions in a year that drag shows were put on in the Grosvenor, but it also acted as a lure for the unfortunate person who found himself outside rather than within the bar, seemed to turn your brain into a heat-seeking missile and itself into a point of perfect heat.

Try it yourself if you don't believe me. Try walking along Little Western Street in the twilight, hearing the pub before you see it, and then seeing in the corner of your eye that light of infernal seduction. The seafront is just a few seconds further on down the street, and on a velvety sort of evening it's just possible that the prospect of the green half-light and calm seas might keep your feet moving, but chances are you'll feel yourself instead falling sideways, pubward. This is perhaps why that door is left open in drinking hours, to prevent cuts and bruises in your involuntary haste to be inside rather than out. At any rate, I learned early on in my summer in Brighton that you didn't walk lightly down Little Western Street after midday; after dark was fatal. And so, if you had work to do or errands to run, people to see, vows of abstinence to keep or books to write, you devised a route which avoided the pub.

If, on the other hand, your mission was drink and stories, inside the Grosvenor was the place to be. There were plush banquettes no one sat in, an upright piano no one could play, a fruit machine to park pints on and a mantelpiece to prop your elbows on. There was a noticeboard pinned with a chaotic montage of snaps from legendary piss-ups, and a glossy ceiling of marigold yellow which reflected the crowns of drinkers' heads; there were framed publicity shots of actors and actresses on the walls, fine Sussex bitter and piquantly bloody bloody Marys behind the bar.

There was all of Brighton drinking there. Airline cabin crew and antique dealers, carpenters and gents' outfitters, nursing home superintendents, electricians and actors, hairdressers, artistes, dog walkers, accountants, bishops' lovers, hoteliers, fiddle players and drunks, heterosexuals and homosexuals, gays who looked straight and straights who looked gay, butch lesbians and sweet *gamines*, randy dogs and supercilious cats. I only ever saw this collection of characters in the pub, half lit-up, so they became the players in a thousand stories. Their outside lives, as embellished and novelized by alcohol and bravado, were allegories of the human condition: hilarious, futile, ironic, tragic, but never quite so bad that a drink wouldn't bring things round.

Sometimes you got dragged into a story yourself and when you finally woke up out of Brighton, somewhere back in the rest of England, you wondered whether it had been true, or whether someone had been stringing you along; or even, perhaps, if you had been stringing other people along. And then you realized that it didn't matter. Brighton was the sum of its stories. There were old stories – crinolines and cat-gut condoms – and public stories – mods and rockers and dirty weekends – and as many private stories as pebbles on the beach, for everyone you met had a yarn about Brighton. Everyone got worked up at the mention of the place, saw seagulls wheeling, saw again the glittering light, and called up a sinuous narrative in which, likely as not, sex hung heavy in the air.

The summer I spent there became another story, became

this book. I came to Brighton to hear its stories, and to write my own – to add another pebble to the cairn of the beach. Sometimes I found myself appropriating other people's tales, and even speaking in their voices. Sometimes I was on the edge of what I understood. Here, on the border between land and sea, in the sea frets and the summer haze, reality hovered slightly off the ground.

Even if you are the sole source of a story, and you keep it under your hat, it escapes somehow, it leaks out from beneath the brim; especially in a pub, especially in the Grosvenor. Stories whizzed around that bar because it was small and because people didn't sit down but pressed together in the centre of the floor and those banquettes remained unoccupied except by the occasional passing stranger who tended to look on in amazement at the regular throng. But it wasn't just the cramped state of the bar which threw people together: the Grosvenor crew were half-mad for gossip, suffered from a collective virus of conviviality, so that every day in there had the euphoric atmosphere of happy hour on an early Friday evening.

It was on a real Friday that I first met Fredda. Standing up by the bar, shouting to make myself heard, I happened to become involved in the same conversation – on liposuction, or Steve Coogan, or the Brighton Trunk Murders – as a glamorous woman of late middle age, whose voice came up sweetly from her diaphragm like water from a well. The conversation subdivided and we found ourselves talking exclusively to each other. And as we talked I recognized her – she appeared in two of the photographic portraits of actors and actresses on the walls. Some I had recognized as youthful studio shots of now familiar faces, such as John Alderton and Wendy Craig, but I had been unable to put a name to her. She told me she was called Fredda Hayworth. I guessed the pictures on the walls had been taken about twenty years before. In fact they were at least thirty years old, Fredda said. Could I not tell from the beehive hairdo? 'The general dolly-bird look, darling.'

Fredda bought me a drink because she meant me to listen. She had posed and pouted for those pictures at the height of a fleeting, cultish fame. In the sixties she was the switchboard girl in *Z Cars*. She was blonde and winning and, most importantly, the script had given her a memorable catchphrase. When she radioed from police headquarters, known as Base Depot or BD, to Colin Welland and Brian Blessed in their Ford Zephyr patrol car she spoke in a sing-song code: 'BD to Z Victor One. Come in Z Victor One.' Fredda now claimed it wasn't just luck which had seen this line undergo that unfathomable alchemy of popular culture whereby thousands of people – on buses, in bars, on production lines – started repeated it, shouting, 'BD to Z Victor One' through cigarette smoke and gloomy mornings.

Luck, her arse. She had approached the role of switchboard girl with the diligence of a method actress, paying several visits to police stations and to the telephone exchange at Kirkby on Merseyside to watch how the girls there worked. She had noted how, irrespective of any regional accents they may have, telephonists – like newspaper vendors or market traders – had a distinct linguistic signature, a method of phrasing which always ended on a rising inflexion. Fredda's 'BD to Z Victor One' was memorably euphonious because she had worked hard to discover the poetry in the phrasing.

The cult status it gave her reached its apotheosis when Bruce Forsyth mimicked her, in front of thousands watching at home, in a live Sunday evening transmission from the London Palladium. 'BD to Z Victor *One*, BD to Z Victor *One*.' Bruce's take-off was a ridiculous exaggeration, rising to a squeak, accompanied by a batting of eyelashes, a coquettish grin, but we understood it, we laughed. Imagine, all round the country, in prefabs and palaces, people laughing because of you. It was a strange kind of feeling. Her eyes glowed in the Grosvenor's orange lamplight.

Time had been kind to Fredda. After they had met her for the first time men tended to play that terrible game with each other. 'Could you . . . ?' 'Yep. I reckon I could. How about you?' 'Yeah. Definitely.' She was still glamorous, still shapely, with that radiance of skin and eyes that is more usually the preserve of youth. But she wasn't working at the moment, age having limited her to the occasional glamorous-granny role, and doubted she would ever work regularly again.

As her acting career slackened off she had started taking in paying guests, renting out rooms to friends and contacts appearing at the Theatre Royal or the Pavilion Theatre or down here on film or television location work. And so by degrees she became a theatrical landlady. 'Ah, so you'll need somewhere to stay,' she said when I explained I was intending to spend the summer in Brighton writing a book.

My plan had been to rent a room in a cheap guest-house where I could come and go, dividing the summer months between London and Brighton. Being drunk by this point, I painted a heroic picture of my needs – a bed, a desk for the laptop computer, a window-ledge for books, a window with quintessentially Brightonian views: rooftops, sea or stucco. 'I'll find a shoebox somewhere,' I said.

'You'll do nothing of the sort,' she said in that deep voice that suggested both water and echo. 'You'll come and stay with me.'

The preening self-regard of the Regency era blew your wig off. It was said, that if you lived for three months in that fresh new Brighton, you would run into anyone you had ever met, and anyone that henceforth you would ever need to know. The season was October to March, when fashionable society decamped here *en masse* – today's equivalent being flying to Barbados on Concorde and spending the winter drinking rum punches and fellating ever fatter cigars with the likes of Michael Winner and Mr Bernard 'Turkey' Matthews. Brunswick Town, comprising Brunswick Square flanked to east and west on the seaward side by Brunswick Terrace, was their all-inclusive resort: a self-contained estate of aristocratic houses of leisure, with elegant façades echoing classical Greece and the Italian Renaissance, surrounded on three sides by fields, with the Downs behind and the ocean in front.

The original colour scheme had reflected that rustic setting, with ironwork painted green, window-frames brown to look like oak, and façades the light brown of hardboard. As the area became urbanized, so the colour of the houses brightened and the ironwork turned black. By now the frontages were that creamy stucco known as Brunswick Cream – the colour of Cornish clotted cream, fading to French mustard as salt and ultra-violet took their toll.

Graham Greene wrote in *Brighton Rock*: 'the cream houses ran away into the west like a pale Victorian water-colour'. But I didn't think that was quite right when – still amazed by my good fortune in running into Fredda – I stood on the seafront and looked towards the windows of my new room. The description didn't do justice to the magisterial vision of the Georgian architects, Charles Augustus Busby and the Wilds, father and son, Amon and Amon Henry: the window bays and porticos, friezes and projecting cornices and Ionic columns, the ironwork railings and lead canopies and classical porches. Above all, the light wasn't a static, wishy-washy light. The light deluged the creamy buildings and they absorbed the power of the light and flung it back out to sea, so the light was dynamized, visionary.

When I stood on the end of Palace Pier and looked back, from Lewes Crescent, Kemp Town, in the east to Adelaide Crescent, Hove, in the west, when I panned my eyes slowly from Shoreham to Newhaven, I saw Turner's light and Canaletto's buildings. I saw a panorama of hallucinatory clarity and splendour. Now – would you believe it! – here I would be, part of this legendary panorama; when I stood at my attic windows in Fredda's house I became an infinitesimal dot on the retinas of admiring onlookers.

Brighton's splendid frontage, the fact that it often conceals decrepitude, has provided a useful metaphor for the town – 'The shabby secret behind the bright corsage, the deformed breast', as *Brighton Rock* has it. It was literally true that this splendour was scarcely more than paint-deep in some cases. A favourite building material of many of the Regency terraces and squares was called bungaroush, a mix of lime and flint using both smooth pebbles from the beach and rough-edged flints from the surrounding fields. Bungaroush became synonymous with shoddy workmanship, as if the property speculators and builders of Regency times were jerrybuilders and fly-by-nights who whacked up these apparently grand edifices any old which way.

Bungaroush was a very Brightonian concept. The word sounded dashing but bogus, an ostler from Patcham masquerading as a Levantine prince. By reputation it looked the part but fell to bits, like a rocking chair you might buy from a knocker-boy in a pub near the station. It was true that some bungaroush was of poor quality – when you knocked in a picture hook and heard the rubble shifting and dropping, a sound like mice scurrying – yet its reputation was generally undeserved. Perhaps because of its name, bungaroush was whipping boy for more than a century and a half of weathering and ageing.

Then again, many of the houses were not intended as permanent residences but as furnished properties to be let for the season – the nearer the sea, the more likely this was. For much of the nineteenth century, the house now owned by Fredda was listed in the annually updated *Brighton Directory* as a 'Furnished House'. In 1865 it was owned briefly by a Mrs Byam – when her neighbours in Brunswick Terrace included Major-General Sir Adolphus John, Bart; Baron de Teissier; Antonio Arroyave Esq.; and Sir Robert Fitzwygram, Bart – before reverting to rented status.

14

The First World War was a watershed. In the *Brighton Directory* of 1915 not a single house in Brunswick Terrace was listed as having been turned into flats. By 1923 several houses had been converted into self-contained apartments and the process had continued from there, leading to the present predicament of many – lived in by short-stay tenants, For Sale boards up, binbags and bicycles in the basement yards.

This was why Fredda's house was so unusual, so magnificent. Fredda's house had not been cannibalized. Its interiors remained, give or take a bathroom here and a toilet there, more or less as they had been in the 1820s. In fact you may have recognized the interiors if you saw a particular episode of *Lovejoy*, or the (risibly bad) feature film version of *Fanny Hill*, in which, incidentally, Fredda played a madame. The staircase spiralled to my attic room in a series of diminishing rectangles. Round each bend, as I did the climb, I was met with my own mildly perspiring image in a gilt-edged mirror or glazed wall.

The staircase was dim; the doors opening off it into large, high-ceilinged rooms revealed sudden shocking blasts of light. In these rooms the chinoiserie, the paintings, screens and dragons, the chandeliers and marquetry card tables were an echo of the Pavilion. Up in Fredda's bedroom, where she claimed to be one of only two Brightonians to sleep beneath a mosquito net (How did she know? Who was the other? She never said), the original wardrobe bore the fake – but honourably so, early-Victorian – initials of the Prince Regent. The carved canopy above the bed, from which the mosquito net was suspended, had been rescued from a house belonging to an exiled Russian count, scion of the Romanovs.

Before the war the antechamber to the first-floor drawing room had been a casino; the door had a sliding window in it and, next to the grand piano, the floor beneath the carpet was drilled with cigarette burns. This was where the bar had been, rescued from the Royal Albion Hotel when it was refurbished in the 1920s and installed here by former owners and legendary topers Ernest and Mabel Pinecoffin. Having spent so long sitting at the bar when it was in the hotel, the Pinecoffins couldn't bear to be parted from it, so the story ran. Fredda's was a house with an exotic air and history, and down on the ground floor, in the long kitchen, a parrot and two parakeets kept up an appropriately exotic aural motif, their squawks and chirps rising all day long through the cool layers of the house.

Fredda's kitchen was a stage. The parakeets squawked and the front door banged deep into the night with exits and entrances. A Regency cartoon entitled 'A Voluptuary Under the Horrors of Digestion', showing a glutton bursting from his breeches and dripping grease from his slack mouth, held pride of place. Fredda's actorly friends who gathered beneath it were vain and self-obsessed, but often in ways you felt disposed to forgive them for, for they seemed permanently stunned and gladdened by the novelty of narrative. They launched into parallel stories which might or might not intersect.

'Gosh, I haven't been to Margate since, ooh, 1958. I was in *The Gift* in rep there.'

'You were in *The Gift* in Margate in 1958? My God, I thought I recognized you! I played your sister!' (*They embrace, pour more wine, clink glasses*)

They needed, in fact, a good director; for each to have his or her own personal and permanent director following them about, telling them what to do, what to think, what to *emote*, would have been a marvellous and hilarious thing. Brighton was an actorly, theatrical sort of place. There were Larry Olivier and the smoking-jacketed Terry Rattigan, the potato-faced Dame Flora and husky-voiced Edna O'Brien. There were chaps who sat on bar stools with drunken noses and told tales of first night disasters, there were ageing gals who had slept with fame and wealth when fame and wealth were still skint and ugly. There were the brushes with greatness, the insights on immortality.

'The first time I ever said, "Action!" in my entire career, it was to Orson Welles. That's absolutely true. And Orson said to me . . .'

'John Lennon turned to me and said, "Listen, friend, don't worry about Paul, he just wants to be Cliff Richard." As I sit here, that's God's own truth.'

In my early days in Fredda's house I kept them company, if invited, but I soon learned that you didn't need to be there to know what was being said. My fellow-boarders, usually actors down for a week of performances in one of the two main theatres, occasionally put in an appearance. But having been on stage all night they didn't need another stage. The greasepaint was off, the soul was flat, they had curiously little to say. Was this what my new-found, gregarious and garrulous friends were like when they eventually got home to Hove or Kemp Town or Hanover Crescent? Did they hang up their characters on a hook?

Early in my stay Fredda gave sanctuary to a dancer with injured leg and pride. She had received a call from the director of a production of *42nd Street* at the Theatre Royal. One of his principal female dancers had gone lame and needed molly-coddling. He proposed taking her out of her anonymous, lonely hotel bedroom, where she had too much time in which to imagine her understudy putting in barnstorming performances, and placing her with a sympathetic landlady. 'Of *course* she must come here,' Fredda had said, thrilled at the prospect. When I called by chance from London the next day to confirm a visit, she said: 'Your timing is immaculate, darling. I have the most gorgeous, exotic creature staying here. People are finding all kinds of excuses to call round, just for a look.'

Travelling down on the train, I amused myself in imagining the gorgeous creature. It was interesting that, with her own looks faded, Fredda could still admire this woman of probably less than half her age for the power of her physical presence. Weren't faded beauties supposed to be sad and mad, like Norma Desmond? Then again, Fredda hadn't described her in terms of womankind. The image that recurred was of a larger version of the parrot in the cage in the kitchen, a freakishly large bird with iridescent plumage.

I imagined this bird trapped in the first-floor drawing room, shifting about on its injured leg between the grand piano and the Chinese wall-hanging, backing into the ancient wooden cine camera, panicking and flexing her wings, sending the chandelier swinging madly and reflecting blue and green panels of light across the ceiling. And the noise, the squawking! Fredda clapped her hands in delight at the spectacle, quite forgetting about the injured leg, the distress. There was a queue of people lining the stairs, hoping for a glimpse, covering their ears at the squawks. There were more people in the road outside, heads back, gazing at the drawing-room windows, shepherded by a long-suffering policeman with a megaphone. Paparazzi with bazooka-sized zooms were up stepladders . . .

But there were no crowds outside Brunswick Terrace when the taxi dropped me there. All was silent as I let myself into the house. Fredda was in the kitchen at the back and though she didn't actually bring her forefinger to her lips to indicate the necessity for absolute quiet, she did, without realizing it, speak in a whisper. 'The dancer', she said, 'is resting. Worn out, poor girl. We'd best not disturb her.'

I felt let down but Fredda suggested she might rally in the late evening and we might share some wine. Before settling down to work, I popped up to Waitrose in the Western Road and bought a nice bottle of Chablis which I left in the walk-in refrigerator. Around 10 p.m. I opened the door of my room and looked down the several flights of stairs which fell geometrically like a study in perspective. A light was on at the bottom but I heard no voices, no popping of corks or deep-throated laughter. I decided on an early night.

Next morning I awoke with the dancer in my head. She had to eat, I reasoned. She would be at breakfast. But as I went downstairs I passed Fredda going the other way carrying a

18

breakfast tray bearing coffee, fruit and croissants. 'She's feeling a bit fragile,' said Fredda. 'The leg stiffened up during the night.'

I had reasons to be out and about that day, but I also found reasons to return to the house, and on my second return visit, in the late afternoon, there she was, the dancer, the fabulous creature, carrying her beauty like an afterthought. She was sitting on a chair in the kitchen, her damaged leg propped on another chair, and she was wearing a short satin gown, belted at the middle, and not a great deal else. The visible leg was extremely long, and suntanned, and her cleavage was deep and cool and shadowy, making me want to cool my wrists there, paddle my ankles, arch my neck. She was called Ana and had a limited command of English.

How was the leg? She tousled the back of her hair and rolled her eyes and said, 'Eet's fucking . . .' She searched for the right word, found it: 'shit.' Still, it was nice to be in Brighton, no? There were worse places to be laid up. She scowled and shrugged. 'If I no dance, eet's shit. In Paris shit, in Milano, shit. In New York, Prague, London, all shit.'

Ana and I did not achieve that stage of conviviality which demanded the broaching of the Chablis. But in general, between Fredda's house, the Grosvenor Arms round the corner and the cheerful bibulous depravity of most Brightonians, there were plenty of opportunities for drinking – too many to be healthy for someone with things to do. And so early on I laid down an apparently simple rule for myself – I should avoid social situations that could be guaranteed to end in drunkenness.

It was, evidently, an age-old hazard of Brighton. On a visit to the Pavilion I came across a satirical cartoon of 1802 entitled *A Brighton Breakfast, or Morning Comforts*. Similar to the cartoon in Fredda's kitchen, it showed the then Prince of Wales's mistress, Maria Fitzherbert, and her friend Lady Lade, seated at the breakfast table and pigging out on a feast of cold cuts and liquor. Bursting from her bodice, Mrs Fitzherbert was pouring gin from a bottle marked HOLLAND into a glass marked COMFORTS, and saying: 'Won't you take another comforter?' An empty brandy bottle stood next to Lady Lade, who replied: 'I think your comforters are bigger than my John's.'

The satire of *A Brighton Breakfast* was aimed at the follies and excesses – sartorial, culinary and venereal – of the fashionable of the day, certainly, but it also said something about Brighton: that if breakfast here was such a dissolute affair, imagine what the rest of the day must hold in store! I told myself sternly that as far as possible I must, so to speak, avoid all invitations to breakfast from Mrs Fitzherbert and Lady Lade. But this was a shyster lawyer's contract I had made with myself, as I soon discovered.

It was one of those evenings that Brighton rolls like marbles under your feet. It started in an art gallery where it was the opening night of a friend's exhibition. I came down on the train from London and Fredda turned up, looking terrific in a black cocktail dress. We drank the cheap white wine and she said this was the kind of do to which, thirty years ago, she would have worn a mini skirt and accidentally on purpose flashed her knickers. At 10 p.m. we caught a taxi to the Grosvenor where, recklessly, we drank the pub's own white wine. At this point things started to grow hazy.

At about 10.20 the pub emptied temporarily, as it tended to do on a Friday, while the clientele went round the corner to the Oriental to catch the drag show there. The Oriental was an exclusively gay bar that grew adhesive with bare-armed, sweaty bodies on Friday nights. Fredda said, 'Let's go for ten minutes. Don't *worry*, I'll look after you.' The drag show had finished by the time we got there and the small stage in the corner had been turned over to karaoke. A young boy caught in the crossfire of coloured spotlights was getting a huge ovation for a falsetto version of 'Happy Talk' from *South Pacific*.

Old queens with pomaded hair sat with their ancient mothers. Everyone roared with laughter, their faces glistening in the lights, their eyes running amid the smoke and laughter. I received a few pats and archly raised eyebrows. Another glass of white wine for Fredda and me – quite good, as I remember, properly chilled at least – and we were back at the Grosvenor. It was at this point, as I perched on the bar stool and clung on to the bar-top as if I were in a crow's nest and the linoleum far below were a pitching deck, that Fredda mentioned Frank Windsor.

Frank, best known for his roles in *Z Cars* and *Softly Softly* in the 1960s and '70s, had been staying the week at Fredda's whilst appearing at the Theatre Royal. In my lit-up state, the idea of Frank Windsor staying in the same house seemed unbearably exciting. Frank had been an early hero of mine for his role as first Sergeant, then Inspector, Watt in *Z Cars* and later in *Softly Softly*. He created a memorable chemistry with Stratford Johns, who played Superintendent Barlow, the bruiser to Frank's tough but fair sidekick. Watt's character was unabashedly northern, part of that gale of believable characters with recognizable accents that blew so bracingly through British sitting rooms in the 1960s. In fact Sergeant Watt was a trailblazer for any number of lesser lights who have dimly illuminated the world of television coppers in the thirty-odd years since he first appeared.

There was another reason why Frank Windsor meant something to me. I had a particular memory of a long-ago Christmas Day when it snowed and, most happily, one of my presents was a toboggan, and a special episode of *Z Cars* was shown on Christmas morning when daytime television was still a rarity. My memory was of the world being ordered, harmonious and benign in a way in which it would seldom, if ever, seem to me again – and Frank had been part of this little piece of heaven I was privileged to glimpse.

'Do you think he would like a drink?' I asked Fredda,

swaying at the bar. 'Please tell him I'll buy him a drink. I owe him one.' I didn't think he would come. Fredda seemed doubtful but popped back to the house anyway to ask him. By now it was well after closing time, the door was locked, the lights dimmed and the curtains pulled carefully across. A man at least as drunk as me told me all about a perpetual motion machine he was about to put the finishing touches to. He went into it in great detail – something to do with magnets, hence no friction – and grabbed a beer mat in order to draw a diagram, though happily a pen could not be found and he presently forgot what he was doing and wandered off.

I ordered a final glass of lukewarm, corrosive wine and expected to see no more of Fredda that night, let alone Frank Windsor. But ten minutes later there was a feathery tap on the glass of the door, someone opened it and in walked Fredda, followed by Frank.

Try as I might I can remember practically nothing about meeting Frank Windsor. He was dressed, I think, in tweedy hues, green and brown – or was I confusing that with the fertilizer commercials he appeared in on afternoon television? He was shorter than I had imagined, and he walked into the pub not with the casual confidence of a Sergeant Watt, but with a hesitant lope, blinking in the fug. I managed, at least, to resist the near-overwhelming temptation to burst into a whistled rendition of the *Z Cars* theme tune when I saw him.

He sat facing me on a bar stool and his face was the same, the enquiring but kindly terrier, and I know I bought him a drink. I told him that he was an icon of post-war Britain, I became insistent on the point. I banged the bar-top, I toasted him with my glass of dreadful wine. 'A bloody icon. I'm telling you.' To which, with a long-suffering, lopsided grin and the bluntness of Sergeant Watt, Frank had replied: 'Don't be so bloody ridiculous, I'm just a jobbing actor.'

This must have been but one of the prize specimens of bull-shit which Frank so charmingly put up with, for the evening did not, apparently, end there, at the bar of the Grosvenor, with a last dose of house paintstripper. The next morning when I woke up in my attic room, with the light streaming off the sea and in through the windows, the fragmented memory of the previous night began to pulse about my stricken brain, and it dawned on me with horror that I had insisted on opening another bottle when we got back to the house.

I opened the Chablis I had bought for the exotic and foul-mouthed Ana, my excuse being that I needed a drink of something decent to take away the taste of the rubbish I'd been drinking all night. But the real reason was to extend the evening long enough to tell Frank about a snowy Christmas long ago when I had never been happier. Perhaps I had even shed tears . . . Oh Christ. I left a note in the kitchen and crept out of the house before Frank or Fredda had got up, too embarrassed to face them.

It was an important lesson Brighton had to teach: that it takes more than a casual resolution to combat its endlessly inventive genius for getting you shit-faced.

Chapter Two

Slow-witted and clumsy, the natural butt of jokes, Billy Masters wasn't your typical Brightonian. We were first-years together at a boarding school in the Sussex countryside. It was a charity school, founded for orphans and paupers and now serving the children of the lower middle classes who had fallen on hardish times for one reason or another. The business of boarding didn't run in the family or the genes and came as an icy shock after the bourgeois verities of Wimbledon or Redhill or, in Billy's case, somewhere rather grandly shabby and leafy off Dyke Road, Brighton.

I remember, in the first few days at school, asking a master a question, a perfectly reasonable enquiry about mealtimes or table tennis, and being told to look on the noticeboard, being asked in disbelief if I had not *noticed* the noticeboard. From now on we were surnames and numbers in a quasi-military bureaucracy and we were often made to feel as if we were infuriating hindrances to the smooth running of that bureaucracy. If only there were no ghastly little oiks, with their asinine enquiries and ill-fitting new clothes, the system would run perfectly! And so it was the function of the system to break us down into manageable and obedient component parts of the big, implacable machine.

Those early days were dark, literally so, for much of the time. We were woken in darkness at five to seven by the clanging of a bell. A master would come into the dormitories, flick on

24

the rows of bare lightbulbs and rouse us from dreams of home by kicking the ends of our iron bedsteads. We had twenty minutes to wash and dress and be on parade on the asphalt outside for roll-call. Then, to barked orders from a duty monitor, we marched in ranks of four, military fashion and still in darkness, the quarter-mile to the dining hall for breakfast. 'Squad, squad, *'shun*! From the right, number . . . Form fours. Right turn! By the left, quick *march*! *Left*, right, *left*, right, *left*, *left* . . .' Square-bashing before sunrise – later it would seem ludicrous, yet we also marched to lunch, to the accompaniment of the school brass band – twirling maces and *oompah* brass – as if every day were a passing-out parade at Sandhurst.

It was the marching that first fingered Billy Masters as lacking the basic requisites for survival in this Darwinian forcing house. In the classroom and on the rugby field he was merely averagely useless, but when it came to marching he was uniquely and hilariously incapable. Presumably the part of his brain that controlled motor functions was less developed than it might have been, for the impression was that his brain was wired up wrongly to his legs. When he took a step forward with his left foot, his left arm swung forward also; his right foot and arm behaved likewise. It was an involuntary movement and it seemed there was nothing he could do to prevent it. But God, was it funny! He looked like an ape! He lumbered like a primate!

It was doubly funny because not only did it make us laugh, but Billy Masters would be punished for failing to achieve the standard of marching required and expected by the school, and his punishment would be – more marching! Every evening the housemaster would take him out on to the asphalt and drill him for fifteen minutes while we looked on from the windows of the day room, watched him blundering miserably about like a junior Frankenstein's monster. Our housemaster – a chain-smoking bachelor whose usually mild stutter became uncontrollable when he was obliged to talk to boys' mothers – mocked and bullied Billy Masters between puffs on his Senior Service: 'Left, Masters, *left*, *left*, right, *left*, right . . . Good God, boy. Are you d-deaf, or stupid, or b-both?'

We were all enormously indebted to Billy, had we but known it. Billy taught us that however miserable and bewildered we may have been, however yearningly we dreamed of our mothers and our own bedrooms, someone was worse off than us. We transferred all our own miseries on to Billy and then, following the example of the housemaster, we punished him for carrying such a burden. We were inventive in the ways we found to hurt Billy Masters. We drew a bra on his blubbery chest in indelible felt-tip pen. We forced him to eat a pot of mustard. We intercepted letters from his mother, read them out to him in mocking voices then burned them. We intercepted the cakes and biscuits she sent and ate them in front of him. In freezing weather, when a stream of piss was needed to shatter the ice in the toilet bowl, we stole the blankets from his bed and made him wear sopping wet underpants.

Then one day Billy disappeared. Official anger at his absence turned to panic as the day wore on and he hadn't returned. Boys were dispatched to search hidey-holes. Masters scurried about looking at their watches. Soon the police would have to become involved, which wouldn't do at all. Rumour was rife. The previous year, before we had started at the school, a boy had hanged himself in the toilets. This had been kept quiet at the time, presumably lest it put off the parents of the next year's intake, and we had not learned of it until we became pupils ourselves. The official version of this occurrence was that the boy had developed a macabre interest in methods of execution, and tried an experiment that went wrong. But even at the age of eleven we found this hard to believe. We reckoned that the boy had done it because he was unhappy. This was much more believable.

Perhaps Billy Masters had killed himself too, which was also believable. As twenty-four hours passed with no sign of Billy, what had started as speculation hardened into near-certainty. Billy Masters had killed himself! No one knew where, but we were sure he had done it. It was just a question of someone eventually stumbling across his body. After the initial shock and excitement at the notion of Billy's suicide, we began to feel guilty. If Billy had been unhappy, who had made him so? By the second day of Billy's absence, with the masters refusing to give us any information, a cloud of collective depression had settled upon us.

Then, that evening, the housemaster called a special meeting in the day room. We shuffled into the room in a state of silent tension. The housemaster, drawing so hard on his cigarette he whistled as he inhaled, looked grim too. But when he spoke, it was to tell us that Masters had returned. When we went up to the dormitory we would see him there in bed. 'And I will not have boys talking to him, asking him questions, feeling s-sorry for him. Masters has done wrong. He has to learn that this s-sort of transgression will not be tolerated. The boy must have solitude in which to c-contemplate the gravity of his offence. And now if you will join with me in the Lord's Prayer . . .'

Masters lay in bed with the bedclothes pulled over his head. The bed moved now and again with his silent sobs. He knew he had been officially sent to Coventry and we didn't dare try to speak to him in case the patrolling housemaster caught us doing so. We readied ourselves for bed in near-silence, put on our pyjamas, turned down our beds, queued to use wash basins and toilets in orderly fashion. Slowly our subdued behaviour assumed the qualities of a silent protest. The housemaster, when he came into the dormitory, tried to jolly us up, as if nothing had happened. We just smiled ruefully at him and carried on brushing our teeth or reading our books. The house-master grew visibly annoyed. 'Right,' he said. 'An early night will do us *all* good.' And he snapped off the lights fifteen minutes early. The silence continued for many minutes,

27

seemed to stir itself slowly into the blackness until the two were indivisible. Then a voice pierced this dark silence, speaking for us all. 'Hey, Masters. Psst. Billy. *Billy!* Where've you been? Where'd you go?'

'Brighton,' whispered Billy Masters. 'I went to Brighton.'

As marching had been Billy's downfall, so escape became his redemption. He had found the thing he was good at. We all wanted to escape. We all gazed beyond the perimeter fence, saw the roofs of nice little bungalows, saw ordinary people going about their business, saw, in fact, little facsimiles of the comfortable world we had so recently come from. We all wanted to be there on the outside rather than here on the inside. But no one except Billy did anything about it. He became an inveterate escaper, but these weren't impulsive, hysterical dashes across the green fields. He was cold-eyed, biding his time, and when he glimpsed a chink of possibility he'd be off, swift and silent. When Billy bolted our hearts went with him, and while his freedom lasted we walked a foot off the ground.

Billy's means of escape were various and resourceful – buses, trains, bicycles, thumbing lifts – and his goal was always the same, always Brighton. Once there he would make a beeline for the seafront. There was no question of going home. His escapes were also escapades, fantasies. In Brighton he could lose himself. I would wonder precisely what he got up to in his few snatched hours there, while we were in double Latin or making Airfix Spitfires, and I suppose most of the time he had so little money he just mooched about enjoying his unaccustomed freedom and anonymity, letting the ocean light hit the back of his eyes.

After one jaunt, for which I had lent him money in return for a full debriefing when he got back, he told me he had met a man from the secret service who had led him on to the beach beneath the Palace Pier, where the crashing of the sea sounded like cymbals, and taken down Billy's details in a notebook:

name, address, age, height, weight, hobbies. The man had said he reckoned Billy might be secret agent material, but he would need to complete the formality of a thorough medical examination. He suggested they wander up the beach and find a more private spot. At this point Billy had had the nous to make his excuses and get the hell out, though he still wanted to believe that the man was genuine. 'P'raps,' he said as he whispered the story to me in the changing rooms, 'I could get a note from the school quack saying I'm OK, then this bloke wouldn't need to examine me.'

It would grow dark, and Billy would grow cold and hungry, and eventually there would be nothing for it but to leave the seafront and return to the house he had shown me pictures of, gothic and rambling, to face the music. His parents, already notified by the school that he was on the loose, would be waiting. His mother would be in tears. His father, for whom Billy's unhappiness at school betrayed a lack of moral fibre, would thrash him with a belt and drive him back to school where, with parental approval, the housemaster gave him a second belting with a Dunlop Green Flash gymshoe and sent him off to the dormitory with no supper. This is where we would find him and where, despite strict instructions not to talk to him, we would try to be kind.

So this was what I first knew of Brighton. The pictures Billy painted of his time there chimed happily with a conceit that had taken root when I was very young. My grandmother, whom I remembered as little more than a scented polka-dot dress, died when I was three. She had lived with us and her sudden absence was baffling. She couldn't have gone far because her shoes were still in the cupboard under the stairs. My mother explained gently that Gran had gone to heaven. Heaven sounded familiar. I puzzled over the place name for a while and then I remembered where it was. Heaven was where people went on their summer holidays. Heaven had beaches and blue sea. I had this image of Gran, still in her spotty dress, sitting under a beach umbrella having the time of her life. And so, through a babyish confusion of heaven with Devon, I was introduced in the gentlest possible way to the idea of death.

Now I bracketed Brighton with Devon. But Brighton wasn't death, Brighton was freedom from marching in step. When Billy bunked off to Brighton in those November and December days of the final year of the 1960s, and we were introduced to rugby on bone-hard pitches, and the water froze in the toilet bowls, I imagined Brighton to be a place balanced in year-round summer, bathed in sunlight and warmth.

Billy Masters learned to curb his compulsion to escape, learned the craft of survival. At sixteen he failed all his O levels – intentionally, I liked to think – and was finally removed and sent to a local comprehensive in Brighton. I had never become a particular friend, and as far as I was concerned that was the end of Billy's story. But there was a postscript. Some five years later, when I was a student, I was walking along the seafront past the bottom of Regency Square, on my way to visit a friend who was studying at Sussex University and had a bedsit in Hove.

It was the spring bank holiday and the sun was shining; on my right was the cream stucco and caramel brickwork of Regency Square, on my left the dazzling silver of the sea. As I walked along my eyes were drawn to a shocking-pink car parked on the south side of the square. It was an open-topped, 1950s American gas-guzzler, and as I registered its space-rocket lines I became aware that there was a figure lounging in the back seat, using the car as a kind of park bench with knobs on on this boulevarding spring day, and that this figure looked familiar.

I risked a more direct look and found myself staring at Billy Masters. He had lost the puppy fat that had stayed with him into adolescence, he wore wraparound shades and a Hawaiian shirt, and he looked pretty hip. But it was Billy all right. It was as if the character I saw before me was a brilliant kidder and the old Billy – the *young* Billy, the boy who couldn't march, the boy we forced to eat a pot of mustard, the boy who escaped – just one of his many plausible creations. And as I hurried by – face averted, too confused to confront the past head-on – it struck me happily that Billy had learned an important lesson, the lesson Brighton had for us all: why march when you could swank?

By the time I saw the slimline, cool-cat Billy in his finned car I had visited Brighton several times and its status as an imaginary place, a state of mind, had been overtaken by reality. The first time was when Roedean School, the posh gels' academy high on the cliffs in Rottingdean, inadvisedly invited our sixth form to a pre-Christmas disco. The coach that took us there hung heavy with sexual expectation and excitation, not to mention the whiff of Brut and sebaceous secretions. Exposed on its hillside, battered by gales and meanly windowed, the school looked like Colditz, we all agreed; except that our mission was to get in, as it were, not out. The task in hand was to breach the girls' defences, get past the brassières and knickers. What then? We hardly knew. For six years we had barely seen girls, let alone touched them.

As we arrived in the car park a pointed window creaked open and a voice squealed: 'Miss. *Miss*! They're here!' A youth called Danny, a frightening sod from the Isle of Dogs way, was first off the coach. In his platforms and flash togs he flung out his arms towards the girl at the window and breathed deeply of the briny air. 'I smell fanny!' he declared.

The Roedean disco was our way of discovering what all men learned, south of the Thames and east of the Solent: that Brighton meant sex. Not just any old sex, either, but what we stupid, sexist men were taught was the best kind, casual and guiltless, the sort you got from scrubbers or toffs or foreigners, those who didn't know better, those you would never marry. Heartened by our relative success in finger-fucking the toffs we turned our attentions to foreign-language students, with which

Brighton was blissfully awash, and spent Saturday afternoons shambling around the Lanes and up and down the seafront staring hopefully at Swedish girls.

Oh those blond plaits and Scandinavian morals! Foreigners were a different proposition from the poor old inmates of Roedean. Here were girls who had been cavorting naked in mixed saunas since they were knee high to a smorgasbord. Our sexual rites of passage had consisted of trying to hold down involuntary hard-ons whilst marching along to 'Colonel Bogey'. After running the gamut of rejection, from being laughed at to being walloped in the knackers by a clog, we took to drinking in the back bar of a pub on the seafront called Dr Brighton's. It was a recuperative place, dingy as the inside of an old Gladstone bag, with a touch of the startling, for on the ceiling beams were painted pithy sayings: MARRIAGE IS A GREAT INSTITUTION – FOR THOSE WHO LIKE INSTITUTIONS, YOU WILL NEVER PERSUADE A MOUSE THAT A BLACK CAT IS LUCKY.

There we sat, drinking to keep our spirits up, our eyes periodically drawn upward to those salutary inscriptions. When I think back, another saying materializes on the beams: SWEDISH SEX BOMBS AND NORWEGIAN NYMPHOMANIACS DO NOT SIMPLY THROW THEMSELVES AT YOUNG BOYS – NO, NOT EVEN IN BRIGHTON.

Twenty years later I walked into Dr Brighton's again. It was the place I remembered best in Brighton and later I had been gratified to discover that it had a literary significance. When I drank there the front bar had also comprised a reception desk for a hotel called the Star and Garter, whose rooms were above. Sixty years ago both the hotel and the bars had been called the Star and Garter, and it was this establishment Graham Greene had had in mind for the pub which features in the opening pages of *Brighton Rock,* though he didn't give it a name.

Here, standing in the deserted lounge bar, Fred Hale was confronted by the men who were about to kill him, and looked longingly – through a glass partition and across the ladies-only saloon bar – at the big-breasted Ida Arnold in the public bar, singing ballads in her rich Guinness voice. Thirty years after *Brighton Rock*, in *Travels With My Aunt*, Greene mentioned the Star and Garter by name and described those 'inscriptions of a philosophic character', though he placed them on the walls, not the beams. At some point in the 1970s the pub had officially taken on the name Dr Brighton's, by which it had been known in any case – before the war there had been a poster outside listing the 'consulting hours' and the 'prescriptions of the finest quality' to be had within. Dr Brighton was the name coined for the town by William Thackeray in honour of its bracing, restorative properties and thus an excellent choice. In the nearly twenty years I was absent, the pub had come to represent Brighton itself. In my mind's eye I saw that back lounge bar, the engraved mirrors and glass doors, the dark panelling, the gold lettering on the beams, heard the seagulls outside, and knew where I was.

After two decades away, I returned to Brighton on a whim. I had been due to go to Vietnam for the newspaper I worked on but the trip was cancelled with twenty-four hours' notice. How to fill this unexpected gap in my schedule, how to compensate for not seeing the land of napalm and croissants? For no apparent reason Brighton drifted into my head. It was April and the annual arts festival was coming up, which was as good a peg as any on which to hang an article about the place. I had my own youthful memories, for purposes of comparing and contrasting, I had a friend who had recently moved there and who would give me a floor to sleep on for a couple of nights and provide first-class seaside drinking company. So I stowed my passport and coffee-stained copy of *Dispatches*, and went back to Brighton, this time with a notebook.

I drove over from Hampshire on a morning of grey skies and squalls. This approach – sideways, via the A27 which cuts so monstrously through the bald downs behind Shoreham and Portslade – was not propitious. There's only one real way to go to Brighton and that is by train, rehearsing the umbilical link between London and her racy nautical offspring. I parked in the underground car park beneath Bartholomew Square and walked on to the front feeling depressed. Brighton looked like any other seaside resort in grey, off-season weather. The fairy lights strung between lampposts swung in the wind. The Palace Pier was empty, the West Pier, now entirely cut off from the shore, as forlorn and picked over as the carcase of a bird. I saw Dr Brighton's and crossed the road towards it as if it were a life raft. That snug old bar would rescue me, restore my faith, as it had done all those years ago.

I pushed at the side door, and walked into an utterly changed world. The separate bars had been knocked into one large, L-shaped room. The beams had been painted over in garish green, the pithy sayings obliterated, gone for ever. In one corner was a small platform covered in gold tinsel and above it a poster advertising forthcoming drag acts. The barman, who had bleached hair and several studs and rings about his face, had vaguely heard of the inscriptions on the beams. 'Oh, yeah,' he said. 'A long time ago, wasn't it? Someone did mention it.' *Mention* it? If I hadn't already made an arrangement to stay with my friend Roger I would have turned round and left Brighton there and then.

But I had no right to expect the place to be as it was, a formaldehyde version of the Brighton I knew in the mid-1970s. Besides, for every Dr Brighton's there was an example like the Cricketers in Black Lion Street, still a capsule of Edwardiana – bordello-red velvet, 78s stuck to the ceiling, framed sheet music ('"Pucker up and whistle" sung by Florrie Forde'). The seafront, in my day a dispiriting ribbon of tarmac, was in the process of a ritzy transformation, with sweeps of paving, a wooden boardwalk, smart cafés; the North Laine area was a souk of alternative merchandise – 'vegetarian shoes', book-shops specializing in 'mystical geometry' and 'Native American Indian creation stories'; there were fire jugglers in the Lanes and strange drummers down on the beach. Yet it was the same place. It was the beginning of a realization that Brighton has a rare genius for moving with the times yet remaining the same.

I started my researches for the newspaper article in a low-rise flat in Moulescoomb, off the Lewes Road, an area of sink estates reckoned to be as grim and violent as any in Britain. My hostess was the charming heirloom of a bygone age. Daisy Noakes, born 1908, was blind now after a lifetime of domestic service, of sewing buttons and dusting pelmets. She had shrunk to essentials, her skull as beautiful, spare and ravaged as the bird-like curves of the West Pier. The eyes which had seen drunken soldiers, on leave from the trenches of the western front, slumped like sandbags on Brighton seafront, were milky blue as the Channel sky. After the war, when families were being encouraged to breed to replenish the population, her mother had earned a willow pattern dish from the government for having ten children. Daisy overheard her mother saying to a neighbour, 'If someone asked to adopt one of them, I'd have to think hard about which one to give away.'

Daisy remembered the fashion parades between the piers on Sunday afternoons: 'Everybody out in their best, in long dresses and parasols, the beaches so packed it was almost a job to find a pebble to spare.' True Brightonians, she said, took their simple pleasures on the Palace Pier and stayed in its environs. The West Pier was for visiting lords and ladies, who stayed for the season in the grand terraces and squares of Hove.

In a basement flat in Hove, a lady called Daphne Mitchell raged against the dying of the West Pier – and when I used that expression, borrowed from Dylan Thomas, in the subsequent article Daphne raged at *me* for making her out to be a madwoman.

Oh, but she felt strongly about the West Pier. She worked there from 1956 to 1970, five years before it closed, recalled the full houses in the concert hall, the filming of *Oh, What a Lovely War!* when her friend pinched an invalid chair for a joy ride, afternoon teas with the Palm Court Orchestra, the time Hughie Green made a television commercial there for Tide washing powder and gave her ten shillings for being so attentive. 'I would go there now,' she said, 'if someone would take me out on a boat. And if I sat in that concert hall everything would come flooding back. The noise, the orchestras tuning up. It got under your skin. And people who left died. I'm not saying they died *because* they left there, but I think something went from their lives.' In Daphne's span the pier went from china cups and doilies to paper beakers and tables swimming with tea. 'It had a touch of class, but then it got the common, tatty touch,' she said. 'It broke my heart.'

My friend Roger had moved down from north London the year before. He bought a flat in a converted house in Sillwood Place, a block back from the seafront, just to the west of the West Pier and near the border with Hove. But in that part of Brighton, as with Fredda's nearby, you don't do anything as simple as buy a flat; you buy into a fabled architectural and social history.

The pointed windows of the house were scalloped in the fashionably oriental style of the 1830s, and Roger discovered that the house had belonged to a celebrated Regency socialite called Cecilia Margaretta Mostyn and husband Bertie, with whom she had eloped. Cecilia was the daughter of Henry and Hester Thrale, who had lived in a house in West Street where Samuel Johnson and Fanny Burney had been their guests. The house no longer existed but in its place stood the former Sherry's dance hall, which featured in *Brighton Rock* and was now a nightclub called Paradox. Roger told me all this with a big grin on his face. This was Brighton. It was like jumping on a rollercoaster narrative that threw you this way and that. And it never quite stopped, just found new directions.

There were oriental echoes all over Roger's neighbourhood. In the 1820s a local botanist called Henry Phillips embarked on a fantastical project, to build an Oriental Garden and Athenaeum, comprising an onion-domed conservatory heated by steam and tall enough to contain palm trees and other tropical giants, surrounded by a library, reading room and museum, and a school for the sciences and liberal arts. It would be approached from the direction of the sea via a street of grand new villas. Though building started, the scheme foundered due to lack of money, leaving odd clues in local names – Oriental Place, the Oriental pub – and strange and tantalizing fragments of Phillips's original dream, derelict domes and archways leading nowhere, like the backgrounds of allegorical Renaissance paintings.

It also gave the area a distinct topographic identity, and the people who lived there a sense of belonging. Layers of architectural styles and income groups had accrued since Phillips's day. There were Victorian villas with black and white pathways of *trompe l'oeuil* cubes and boot scrapers set low into the walls like tiny little sentry boxes. Some had Japanese four-wheel drives parked outside and cascading windowboxes, some were curtained with rags and leaking weeds from cracks. There were Edwardian hotels, tattoo parlours, phone boxes papered with prostitutes' cards – MATURE ATTRACTIVE LADY, NEVER BEEN SEEN, BONDAGE DOM, CP LEATHER RUBBER PVC. NEW NEW NEW!! BLONDE 19 YRS 40DD–26–36 UNIFORMS DOMINATION SPANKING BONDAGE WATER SPORTS TIED 'N' TEASED, BOUND TO PLEASE!! ALL FANTASY'S 1 MINUTE HOVE STATION.

Shimmering, spacy music floated from attic windows. People swung in hammocks and gathered on west-facing front steps to catch the sun's dying rays. North–south streets fell to the sea, smelled of salt, echoed with seagulls. Sometimes the wind came screaming off the sea and swept you off your feet, all but. The sea was always there at the end of them, squeezed between buildings, bright as a window.

It was on the first of my two evenings with Roger that he introduced me to his local, the Grosvenor, which was as crowded and instantly embracing as I would come to expect of it. I fell into conversation at the bar with a gay man, told him what Daphne Mitchell had said about the West Pier, that it was always the posh bit of the seafront, a very genteel, parasols-and-bone-china sort of place. 'It may have been all genteel up on top, dear,' said the man, 'but it was like Sodom and Gomorrah underneath.' By this he meant that the shadowy area beneath the pier, where the beach shelves up towards the promenade and the sun has never warmed the pebbles, had been a popular cruising ground for gay men.

It was a convenient journalistic conceit, this – top of the pier posh, underneath seedy – and I latched on to it, though the idea it expressed was hackneyed. But it served its purpose in the newspaper article. I had enjoyed my few days in Brighton after not going there for twenty-odd years. Some places were difficult to get anything out of as a writer: buttoned up, cold, suspicious. But Brighton was a pushover. In fact she had been *too* good, for after a while I had had to hold up my hands and say, 'Enough! I am too exhausted to meet any more interesting people, hear any more cracking stories, have any more booze. Take me back to dull old England for some peace and quiet!'

But Brighton, evidently, had not done with me. One morning a few weeks later I walked into the newspaper office where I worked to find a postcard sellotaped to my computer terminal. The card had been sent in by a reader in response to a weekly picture competition we ran called 'Where in the World?', featuring an unusual picture of a reasonably well-known place. The reader's answer was correct (The Pinnacles, Nambung National Park, Western Australia) and she duly won the £25 book token for that week. But what interested me, and what had prompted a colleague to tape the postcard to my computer, knowing I had recently written about Brighton, was the painting on the front of the card.

The painting showed two women sitting at a circular table strewn with breakfast things – jar of marmalade, dish of butter, fruit bowl, coffee- and teapots. In the background, in the bay of the window, was a birdcage with a parrot in it. Beyond the window was a vista of greenery, buildings and sea which suggested that the room, or the house of which it was part, was fairly elevated. According to the information on the reverse of the card the painting was called *Breakfast in Brighton* and was painted around 1950 by an artist called Edward le Bas.

In addition to this standard biographical information, the card imparted an intriguing fact. 'This sunlit painting's Mediterranean atmosphere', the card said, 'caused it to be mistitled "Breakfast in Majorca" for some time.' I flicked the card over and looked again at the painting. Though the style seemed French – and the artist's name suggested he might be French – it seemed scarcely believable that anyone could have thought the picture was of anywhere other than England.

It wasn't just the distinctly parochial breakfast clutter – thick brown glaze on the tea- and coffee-pots, butter-coloured bone handles on the knives – or the winged armchair in the right-hand corner, the heavily draped pelmet above the window or the six-lamped Edwardian chandelier with velvet-trimmed shades above the table; what tugged you by the lapels and said, Listen here, cock, this is England or I'm a Chinaman, were the two people having breakfast.

Cups poised in mid-air, the two women sat very near one another yet conveyed an impression of being a million miles apart. They were dowdy and looked demoralized – neither could be bothered to admire what lay beyond the confines of this stuffy room, what appeared to be a fine view on a fine morning. They weren't talking and probably had said scarcely a word since they sat down. You imagined the squeak and scrape of crockery and cutlery, amplifying the embarrassing gulfs of silence, and thought of duty visits to querulous great-aunts. You may have thought, funnily enough, of afternoon tea as much as of breakfast – of Battenberg cake and tiny saucers – but you emphatically did not think of the Balearics.

The painting began to work away at me. I liked it to look at, its composition and quality of light, yet the confusion over its location suggested something else about Brighton. Was it the case that in the 1950s, a time of austerity and pea-soupers, no one could possibly imagine it ever being sunny in England, not *properly* sunny, and that therefore a painting as drenched in morning sunlight as this was *had* to be somewhere Mediterranean? And was it not the case, though we now had the Clean Air Act and the Body Shop, that we English still inhabited a teabag-coloured world and harboured suspicions of brightness and light, both metaphoric and real?

We wore blacks and greys and browns, the full spectrum of used teabags, and lived under grey skies, shadowless and cowed, for much of the year. We joked about a tyranny of light starvation which throttled our souls by degrees. We congratulated ourselves on a climate of variety, saying, 'Imagine waking up every morning and knowing, *knowing*, it was going to be another beautiful day, eighty degrees, not a cloud in the sky – you wouldn't appreciate it, would you? Then we went to Brighton, stepped off the train down Queen's Road, started rummaging in handbags and Pac-a-mac pockets for barely worn sunglasses, felt dormant sweat glands prickle to life in underwear and socks, felt light searing our brains. And after a few more minutes of this, reaching the front, reeling from ocean light, the turquoise ocean, the light zinging off the ocean and pinging off the stucco, the seafront railings hot as towel rails, we said to each other, 'This is too hot for me, this, give me a nice seventy with a bit of a breeze, I could do with a nice lie-down in the shade, and you know what the cure for hot tired eyes is? Used teabags. Let 'em cool off nicely, then pop 'em on your closed eyes, very soothing.'

This painting, *Breakfast in Brighton*, said, It doesn't have to be like that. Certainly it said, This is England, but it also said, This is Brighton, as well as England. Observe closely – light, parrot, turrets and domes, ocean, horizon, escape. Escape!

In the same week that the postcard was sent I went to a party in Maida Vale and met a civil servant who said that he wasn't permitted to talk to me because I was a journalist. This little joke ensured we stood there chatting for several minutes, in the course of which I mentioned Brighton. 'Ah,' said the civil servant. 'When I think of Brighton I think of that bit in *The Wasteland*. I was at University College, and my tutor was Stephen Spender. I remember him explaining it. D'you know it?' We happened to be standing next to a bookcase which contained a copy of the distinctive 1970s edition of Eliot's complete works, with the black, white and grey dustjacket. I handed it to him, saying, 'Show me,' and he turned up the following lines:

> Under the brown fog of a winter noon
> Mr Eugenides, the Smyrna merchant
> . . . Asked me in demotic French
> To luncheon at the Cannon Street Hotel
> Followed by a weekend at the Metropole.

The Metropole was that red-brick-and-terracotta monstrosity on the seafront that appeared in the background of *Breakfast in Brighton*, vulgar handmaiden to the regal Grand. Pre-war, Spender and other intellectual homosexuals would get their kicks by taking navvies to the Metropole for dirty weekends. 'It was quite the thing,' Spender had said to his seminar students.

I had already noticed how writers as disparate as Thackeray and Patrick Hamilton resorted to rhythmic inventories to convey the breadth of life, the variety of people who sought refuge there. We could all play the game. I made my own list: dodgy antique dealers, preening toffs, dissolute heirs apparent, mods, blowsy tarts, effete intellectuals, raging queens, drunken vaudevillians, Mr Eugenides, Stephen Spender, Billy Masters. I updated it: grungy New Agers, psychics, street performers, drag artistes, smack heads, schizophrenics, the whole panoply of

41

non-profit-making counter-culture. You could go on, making endless lists. You could write a book about Brighton that comprised one giant list, chucking in the word 'raffish' now and again.

I began to see my own connection with the people in these lists. What we had in common was not just that we sought something specific in Brighton; it was that we had been driven to seek something there because it was not available elsewhere in England.

I remembered how the *idea* of Brighton, before I ever went there, was of light and happiness, the antithesis of those dark, cold, early schooldays. The idea still held good, only now I was beginning to see Brighton as the antithesis of England. How did England ever produce a town with the fizz, the craziness of Brighton? It was a marvellous mystery – like a family of duffers producing a babe of Mozartian genius.

I went back to Brighton – this time the right way, by train from Victoria. The fast train – fifty-five minutes, one stop, East Croydon – was now called the Connex Express. It was French-owned and the staff wore bright blue and yellow uniforms which earned them the nickname of 'technicolour gendarmes'. This official livery of yellow and blue was repeated on the trains, which made them look like a poor man's Eurostar. Before the train left an announcer said, rather uncomfortably, 'On behalf of the crew I'd like to thank you for travelling Connex Express . . .', as if there were scores of different trains waiting to go to Brighton and we had been so considerate as to choose *this* one, and an old man piped up, to no one in particular, 'He sounds like he's flying a plane.'

I walked out of the station and stepped over a pair of knickers on the pavement. The first thing I did was to make a symbolic promenade of Queen's Road, which becomes West Street at the Clock Tower and leads down to the sea. Another cliché about Brighton was its status as London-by-the-Sea. But it was true. London had decamped here originally and Brighton would always be its younger, prettier cousin. Queen's Road was an unremarkable thoroughfare in itself – a succession of savings banks, solicitors and notaries at the top end, a few pubs and tobacconists lower down – but its significance lay in where it came from and went to.

Look at a Brighton street map, see the way the railway sweeps into the station like electric wires into a junction box, as if it were a constant cultural power supply flowing direct from the capital. Stand on the station forecourt, beneath the old canopy, and see, two-thirds of a mile southward, the pale chevron of the sea. Queen's Road and West Street carry this figurative electric current on to the sea and then carry it back again. I walked it from superstition, as a hippy might follow a ley line.

At its end, where West Street meets King's Road, the sea is framed by the hideous metallic eggbox of the Odeon Cinema on the right, and on the left by the sentimental Victorian confection of the Sheridan Hotel, decorated with nymphs and cherubs and swags of fruit and, high up in triangular pediments, the masks of tragedy and comedy. Craning my neck to gaze at these sad and happy faces I felt suddenly taut, resonating with impressions, overloaded with Brighton. When I reached Roger's flat in Sillwood Place, still feeling dreamy and exhilarated, he said, 'Hah! Put *this* in your book.' He then took me to the Grosvenor, bought me a pint and told me the story of Guil Shakspeare.

Chapter Three

Fishermen were Brighton's aborigines. People didn't know about them or didn't want to know. It was the only issue on which Brightonians seemed small-minded. When I told Fredda, or Roger, or people in the Grosvenor I was interested in the fishermen they said: 'Why?'

I said, 'Because they were here first.' Then the toffs and snobs came along, took a fancy to their quaint little fishing hamlet, and said, Sling your hook. Fishermen's families were forced out of their cottages in the Lanes to slum tenements on the outskirts of town. Even the name was changed: Brighthelmstone to the snappier, easier Brighton.

It wasn't *quite* as simple and one-sided as this, but it wasn't far off. Hands up how many people even knew Brighton had been a fishing town – or that it still was. The first I knew was when I returned to Brighton to write the newspaper article. Walking the refurbished seafront I came across the fishing museum in the arches there. In adjacent arches old salts with shaving-brush hair mended nets and lobster pots and spoke with authentic Sussex accents. The subtly distinct rural dialects of south-eastern and southern England have just about been swallowed up by the all-purpose lazy twang that is called Estuary English. You rarely heard the old bumpkinspeak of Kent or Sussex any more. Hampshire and Dorset would be next. Yet here were these old guys in their blue smocks, mumbling and joking away like the chorus in *Under the Greenwood Tree*.

Until recently the fishing boats had always sailed off the beach, hence the arches. Now what was left of the fleet sailed out of the Marina, to the east, but the fishermen always touched base at the arches. These barrel-vaulted brick chambers smelled of linseed oil and baccy; the walls were hung with old photographs and boats' name boards: SKYLARK, SEA MIST. The men brewed up constantly in a tarnished old kettle and came and went in battered pick-ups. I hung around one afternoon chatting.

They liked the idea of being a closed community with their own traditions and observances. From way back, for instance, it had been the case that at sea men were referred to by nicknames. All of them had these working names but they were shy about letting on, coy as lovers being asked to explain their secret language of endearments. Perhaps it would bring bad luck to tell. They all pointed at each other and said: 'He's called Queer Boy.' I asked if it would be possible to hitch a lift on someone's boat. They squinted at each other. 'Alan'd take you, only his boat's outta the water. Best bet, speak to Queer Boy. Jack.'

'Who's Jack?'

'Queer Boy? Ah, you can't miss Jack.'

I peered into the gloom of the arch. Perhaps he was in there. 'Is he here?'

'No, he's not *here*, but you can't miss him when he is. Drives a red van. Makes hell of a racket. Hear it coming miles away. Can't miss it. Fact, that might be it now.' The fisherman peered from the arch but it was a dustbin lorry making slow, hissing progress from café to café along the esplanade. 'Anyhow, he'll be here soon. Can't miss him.'

I disappeared for twenty minutes, returned. There was a red van parked outside, rusting everywhere. A squat figure in a singlet held a mug of tea.

'Are you Jack?'

He nodded and I introduced myself.

''Noon,' he said affably. Jack had a ten-metre boat in the Marina and went out potting, crab and lobster, every morning, weather permitting. He'd be happy to take me. 'Got wellies?'

In the late eighteenth century, when Brighthelmstone was becoming Brighton, the fishermen were still using the grassy expanse of the Steine to spread and mend their nets. It was their ancient right and privilege, as enshrined in a medieval charter, but the Steine was also used by fashionable swells and gels who liked to swank up and down in trendy but difficult footwear. They caught their heels in the nets, they teetered to the ground, they landed in mud, their perukes flew off. Rotting-fish smells assailed their nostrils (though in truth they protested rather too much on this score, not smelling too fine themselves in those days of cavalier habits of hygiene).

But the fishermen and their wives really should not have laughed, not so loudly anyway. Not those great, gurgling gusts of belly laughter that echoed around the Steine and up and down the front. Not those honking, goose-like exhalations of mirth that shivered the rafters of the half-built, fantasmagoric Pavilion. And the fish, in retrospect, weren't a great idea; hurling those stinking mackerel at the retreating backs of their elders and betters.

Pretty soon they paid for it in spades. In 1821 the toffs got tough, put a fence round the Steine and said it was theirs. In September 1827 the fishermen rioted, outraged by the abuse of their ancient rights. There and then, ninety-three inhabitants of North Street were sworn in as special constables and, outnumbering the fishermen, squashed them flat. One fisherman was sent to the House of Correction at Lewes *pour encourager les autres*; the rest retreated to the beach and, metaphorically at least, have not been in town since.

The process of discrediting them started soon afterwards. They were idle and drunken, they begged aggressively, they roamed the streets at dawn in the vicinity of houses where fashionable parties had taken place the night before, looking for jewellery or money dropped by revellers. The tenements they lived in were ill-ventilated warrens of courtyards, passageways and low-ceilinged apartments. Outside privies overflowed and people slept on top of each other on the floor like fish on the slab. They were scabby and disease-ridden and smelled absolutely disgusting.

In freshly fashionable Brighton the fisherfolk committed the cardinal sin of being poor and dirty, as shocking as being fat with yellow teeth in California's showbiz belt. The dandies who came to Brighton may have owed their wealth, directly or indirectly, through commerce or banking, to the toil of the poor. But the rich didn't need or want actually to *see* the poor, these agents of profit, and generally the possibility never arose, for the squalid massed ranks of the have-nothings lived far away, out of sight and mind, up north. Brighton's industry was not heavy, but service and leisure, dedicated to pleasure and instruction. Brighton's artisans were a new middle class, teachers of music, drawing, languages, writing, fencing and dancing. Brighton was a social conjuring trick: all rich, no poor. The fishermen were spoiling the trick and had better shape up or ship out.

Fishing is an approximate science. Whether fishing for mackerel beyond the Eddystone Lighthouse, or for herring off Seaford, Brighton's luggers and hog-boats netted all sorts of scaly abominations – wolf-fish, golden maid, gold-finny, miller's thumb, thornback, marblefish, weaver, dogfish. If the new and weird Royal Pavilion were on the ocean-bed, these would be the creatures to fin goggle-eyed through its corridors and state rooms.

On one fishing trip, around the time of which we speak, a stocky little hog-boat was innocently going about its business catching herring off Beachy Head. The conditions were good, cloudy with no moon and a smooth sea. The nets were out, and as boat and nets drifted with the tide the skipper and his

47

two mates waited, mesmerized by the whiteness of the distant cliffs in the otherwise profound darkness. They began to crank the nets in, and the teeming herring seemed to borrow the light from the cliffs, flashing white and silver in the lamplight as they were tipped into the hold.

Then one of the nets stuck fast. The winch handle wouldn't crank. Two men got on it and slowly, as they grimaced and puffed, the net rose from the depths. But something was wrong; they had never known such a weight. They peered through the gloom as the net rose clear of the water. It swung like a giant's hammock. Something huge and bulky was in it, thrashing from side to side. They all three hauled the net aboard, shouting, 'Careful now,' and 'Easy does it,' and 'Watch thee fingers.'

What the hell was it? From what they could see it had the head of a huge shark, and the body of a – what? The body was black, bigger than the largest fat man you have seen. Those things might have been legs, or were they fins or tentacles? 'Looks like a damned donkey,' said one. 'Half fish, half ass!' The mouth worked, flashing rows of teeth, the head started to move from side to side, the men stood well back. Herring lay over it and about it. The body began to rock, throwing off the herring.

And then, in a sudden spasm of monumental power, the creature jerked into the air and towards the side of the boat, pulling the net with it, upending the fishermen on the slimy deck. The creature nearly capsized the boat but the fishermen caught the net, dragged it back and set about it with the iron crank handle and pieces of wood. 'Stop!' the skipper ordered when they had quelled the thing. 'Leave it be now.' For he had an idea and, like a torturer who doesn't want to be found out, he was concerned for the looks of his victim. All the rest of that long dark night, as they pulled in the herring nets, they kept an eye on the hideous creature in the corner of the deck as it flapped and writhed, taking its eternity to die.

The fishermen landed the herring on the beach in the early morning, auctioned off the catch, then returned to the boat for the monster. In the bright morning light it was quite astonishingly horrible, like a giant squid with this protuberant, malevolent-looking head and rows and rows of teeth. The fishermen had not seen anything remotely like it, nor heard tell of such a one; never seen something looking so like a work of imagination and so little like a creature of God.

They rubbed their hands with glee and, then and there, hired a trestle table and a tent and set up an exhibition on the beach: SEE THE MONSTER OF THE DEEP! MARINE SPECIMEN NEVER BEFORE SEEN! PHYSICIANS &C HAVE NOT SEEN THE LIKE. Queues formed on the beach, the rich and the good marvelling at the grotesque aberrations of which Mother Nature was capable. Gasping and wide-eyed, their faces told a story as they emerged from the tent flaps. Swarming children spread the news, which presently reached a certain remote corner of sleepy Hampshire.

Here a country vicar lay abed, watching from his window the swallows swarm around the church roof. A sentence came back to him: 'The congregating flocks of hirundines on the church and tower are very beautiful and amusing!' So he had written in one of the journals he kept on the natural history of his village and which posthumously would form part of *The Natural History of Selborne*, one of the most published books in the English language.

A cup of brandy and water stood on the bedside table next to a leather-bound book. He barely had the strength to lift the cup to his lips, but he persevered, breathing hard, knowing it would help with the pain that soon would be the death of him. The brandy and water had been lately delivered by his housekeeper, who had communicated a remarkable intelligence. Apparently at the town of Brighthelmstone, by the sea in the county of Sussex, a monstrous manifestation from the ocean deeps had been delivered on to the beach there by some fisherfolk of the town.

The Revd Gilbert White, though he did not know Brighton well, had walked the chalk uplands of the South Downs many times from Eastbourne to Chichester, had gazed down on the nest of shacks and windmills that Brighthelmstone had been until so lately. He imagined detouring from the Downs to see the sea monster, and he chuckled at the memory of another visit, a real one, he had made to see and tabulate another fabulous creature. The Goodwood Moose! The more he thought of it the more he laughed, though it pained him to do so.

The Duke of Richmond had brought two female mooses from North America. One had died but the second seemed to have adapted to her new environment and caused a sensation among all who saw her comical vastness. White arranged to go and see this gangling, protuberantly lipped quadruped. He took his measuring stick and notebook. But when he got there he was told the moose had taken sick the morning before and died. White felt momentarily furious with the moose for being so inconsiderate. But then hearing that she had not been disposed of, but hung in a greenhouse, he realized he could still carry out his physiographical investigations, in fact could do so unimpeded by the moose happening to take exception to his proddings and pokings.

The moose had been so ingeniously strapped up, by means of ropes under the chin, belly and bottom, that it looked from the outside as if it had just happened to wander into the greenhouse and, having munched some seedlings, would presently wander out again. But inside the greenhouse, there could be no doubt that the moose was dead. Though it was only March and the temperature remained low, putrefaction was in an advanced state. White decided to work quickly but was pretty soon defeated. Now he reached painfully for the book on the bedside table, his own copy of the work which would become one of publishing's first cult classics. He searched for the right entry. Here it was: 'From the fore-feet to the belly behind the shoulder it measured three feet and eight inches: the length of the legs before and behind consisted a great deal in the *tibia*, which was strangely long; but in my haste to get out of the stench, I forgot to measure that joint exactly.'

He began to laugh uncontrollably, rocking in silent hysteria, about to breathe his last. If he had the youth of forty summers before, and the innocence of not having visited the Goodwood Moose, he would be off to Brighthelmstone like a shot. But he knew what the Sea Monster held in store. The Sea Monster meant shattered dreams, and rottenness. So Gilbert White never conferred immortality on the Brighton Sea Monster, as he did on the Goodwood Moose, by writing about it, and the legend dissolved like the carcase, plundered by souvenir hunters in the night, carried off in a thousand directions until nothing remained.

The Sea Monster taught the fishermen a lesson before it went: how to reach an accommodation with the new, rich inhabitants of Brighton. You took them for a ride. And if you couldn't do it with freak-show fish, you did it literally, by packing them on to fishing boats for a quick whizz round the bay and calling it a pleasure cruise, or boxing them into bathing machines, each of which required its attendant and thus gave work to the fishermen's wives. The fishing folk might still spit in the soup of fashionable Brighton, but they learned to carry the soup to table with a subservient smile.

I had a failure of nerve when it came to telling Jack, the fishing skipper, where I was staying in Brighton. I couldn't tell him Brunswick Terrace, lest it mark me out as a spiritual descendant of the fops who had tripped over the fishing nets in the Old Steine, so I just said, 'Near Brunswick Square,' and he arranged to pick me up opposite the peace statue, the rather beautiful monument to Edward VII which stands on the seafront road exactly on the borders of Brighton and Hove, at six in the morning.

I heard Jack's van before I saw it, rattling and backfiring through Hove. His mate Wayne straddled the gearstick so I could squeeze on to the bench seat. 'Morning,' I said.

''Nin',' said Jack.

''Nin',' said Wayne.

We turned off the road and rattled along the seafront esplanade, past the paddling pool and the petanque court, the Fortune of War pub and the trendy new cafés, to the fishermen's arches, the heart of old Brighthelmstone, where we took on board large rubber buckets, trays of bait, and teabags. Not a soul was about. Then off to the Marina, via a corner shop in Kemp Town, where Wayne picked up milk for the tea and a newspaper, and a bus shelter Black Rock way, to pick up the third member of the crew, a young lad called Lee who bounced into the back of the van on rubber limbs.

Brighton Marina, spread over 120 acres, is one of the biggest in Europe. The town's tourist literature trumpeted this largely meaningless fact as a virtue. Not only did it have 1,700 berths, but there were cod-Regency yuppie villas, with moorings for yachts in place of driveways. There was factory-outlet shopping, a hypermarket, a multi-screen cinema, restaurants and pubs. It was a monument to the post-industrial, post-urban life of the sort sprouting everywhere, except this happened to be by the sea. Having a marina, somewhere to berth and protect boats on this inhospitable stretch of coast, was fair enough, but the rest seemed like a mistake, a miscalculation of the spirit of Brighton. The town didn't need ersatz entertainment, didn't need to follow trends, shouldn't pander to that tired but tenacious phenomenon of yuppiedom.

Having been displaced from their old home on the beach to the Marina, the rump of Brighton's fishing industry, some twelve regularly working boats, were getting sideways looks from the Marina occupants, as their ancestors had done from the toffs on the Steine. They lowered the tone of the place, frankly. Look at Jack's old wreck of a van compared to those sleek German marques parked on the landward side of the yuppie villas. Look at his boat! The Marina was a sea of sleek fibreglass-and-chrome motorcruisers with tinted windows and ostentatious navigational aids. They didn't want Captain Pugwash and his associates spoiling the view with their smelly old tubs. As Jack backfired his way along the Marina's antiseptic boulevards he said sadly, 'We feel like outcasts, that's why we stick together.'

Jack's boat was called the *John Paul*. It had a forecabin with a bench of plastic-covered foam, an echo sounder and navigational equipment, and a gas hob for boiling the kettle. On the salt-smeared window was a sticker that said: NO DOGS OR FAT CHICKS. Behind was a flat deck cleared for hauling in the crab and lobster pots. If you needed a piss you did it over the side. We loaded on the empty rubber tubs, for the day's catch, and the trays of bait. Jack hoicked on his oilskins, looking like a kid in a romper suit. 'What size?' he shouted to me over the throb of the diesel.

'Pardon?'

'Wellies. What size?'

He threw me a pair from the foreward hold and *John Paul* puttered off, an old dobbin, past the sleeping thoroughbred yachts of Sussex's moneyed classes. It had been fine weather all week, warm, bright sunshine, good visibility. From my attic windows I had watched the inshore fishing boats, little potters like the *John Paul*, plying up and down just below the horizon. Through my binoculars I had even fancied I could see the crew members, tiny specks of yellow intent on minute tasks. I had wondered what the view to shore would be like – a completely fresh perspective for a landlubber, unavailable to all but fishermen and yachties. In this light, in this excellent visibility, the entire stretch of the seafront, from Hove to Kemp Town, must present itself like a Georgian panorama of terraces and domes. But today had dawned dull and misty. As we sailed clear of the Marina's concrete wall and pointed out to the open ocean, Brighton appeared as barely more than a smudge off the starboard side.

I watched the seabed deepen on the screen of the echo sounder. It was a strangely dizzying feeling. The bottom of the sea was about sixteen metres down in the Bay of Brighton, then it shelved away until it was fifty or sixty metres in mid-Channel. The sea showed bright orange, as if we were floating on a lake of viscous dye; the seabed was green and jagged. Jack said that crab liked shelving banks with the tide running over them.

Wayne and Lee prepared flounder as bait for the crab, slicing them up, getting their guts running invitingly. The sea was calm as an inland lake; the mist closed in until we sailed in a white cocoon and nothing was visible save a hazy circumference of dark water. Jack made mugs of tea, sweet and strong, the first of several, and read the paper. It was the *Sport*, the only paper he could get, Wayne said apologetically. Jack riffled through it and shook his head.

The fluorescent pink buoys came suddenly out of the mist, marking where the pots lay on the seabed. Jack cut the engine and operated the winch. The crab pots were the shape of Christmas puddings with a funnel in the top. The crabs entered the pot via the funnel, seduced by the promise of eviscerated flounder, then found they couldn't get out. Their only hope then was to be waterlogged, maimed or small. As Jack hauled the pots aboard Wayne quality-controlled the catch. Soggy crabs had flabby undersides, like deflated footballs, and were thrown back. Those on the borderline would go to the Shippam's paste factory at Chichester. There was a big tank there, said Wayne, where the lot went in, shell and claws and everything, and came out the other end as pink paste. He said if he wanted to dispose of a body, that's where he'd put it.

One-clawed crabs also went for paste for, no matter how succulent the flesh of a one-clawed crab, nobody wanted it. Spider crabs, big brothers of the little whizzers you get on a beach, went exclusively to France where they had a taste for them. Some crabs were reprieved for being too small – Wayne measured the width of their shells with an aluminium device and threw back the tiddlers. So he divvied up the catch, chucking crabs in this or that tub, or back overboard. The crabs hit the tubs with a clatter and started trying to climb out, but pretty soon they slowed down, like clockwork toys. Wayne passed on the empty pots to Lee, who rebaited them with slivers of flounder and lined them up ready to be thrown back into the sea. The pots were chucked off the stern of the boat and we went looking for the next pink marker buoy.

Between buoys Wayne picked the crabs up one by one and pushed their claws on to the guard rails on the side of the boat. When the claws opened to grip the rail he used a sharp knife to snip the tendon on the inside. This meant the crabs would be unable to rip chunks out of each other in the tubs. Later, he wound elastic bands tight round the pincers of the lobsters. 'To a lobster,' he said, 'a lobster is food, except during the bonking season. They carve each other to bits. It's a vicious world down there.'

Miscellaneous small fish came up in the crab pots. They were good for either eating or bait, and Wayne chucked them in a plastic tray just near where I stood where they twisted and gasped for several minutes and I tried not to look. My biggest fear, as a matter of fact, was that one of these fish would be so energetic in its attempts to escape that it would flip over the side of the tray on to the deck, and I would be obliged to pick it up and put it back. I've always had an aversion to handling fish. If it had come to it, I suppose I *could* have taken a deep breath and made myself scoop one of these tiddlers back. What came up in the next lot of pots, however, was a different matter.

I saw it writhing as the pot was pulled clear of the water. Wayne was cheered by the sight. 'Ah, tea,' he said. He thrust an oilskinned gauntlet into the aperture and brought it out by the tail, a hideous-looking beast about three feet long. He looked it in the eyes. The creature brought its head up in an arc, flat mouth working silently, showing rows of teeth. Its eyes were slit-shaped and looked like green gelatin. Wayne nodded at it then flung it towards the tray by my feet. 'Dogfish,' he said. 'There's a nice bit of flesh on that.'

Dogfish were part of the shark family. I was watching a small shark flying through the air towards my feet. It was like a man-eating shark in miniature, the blunt art deco snout, the side-mounted eyes, the fuselage-like body. It looked too big for the tray. Surely, at the very least, it would bounce out of the tray and on to the deck. But Wayne had a good eye. The dogfish thumped on top of the other fish, and lay motionless. I relaxed, studied its luminescent brown and grey body. The colours of the rainbow shivered across its body. The cliché about sharks is that they are killing machines; looking at this one it seemed true. Other fish might look like poets or business tycoons, but a shark always looked like a homicidal nutter, with killing on its mind twenty-four hours a day. I was glad this one was dead.

Then it began to move. It raised its head towards me, staring at me with those green eyes, and began to flap its body. At first these were fairly gentle flutterings, but the fish gained strength and ambition. Soon it was slapping its body against the tray as vigorously as a wrestler pleading for a submission. Its body was lifting in the air, and it was surely only a matter of time before it tipped itself over the edge. Jack, Wayne and Lee were busy with the crab pots and were paying no attention to the dogfish. I decided to retreat inside the cabin and read the *Sport*. That way, if the dogfish did escape from the tray I couldn't be expected to retrieve it.

You do not so much read the *Sport* as tot up the number of breasts in amazement. With one eye on the entrance to the cabin in case a dogfish suddenly appeared there, I got to fifty-three before Jack appeared. His mobile rang – an Italian restaurant in Hove with an order for crab. He wrote it down in his notebook, turned the *John Paul* around and we motored back towards the Brighton shore and the lobster fields.

The mist was lifting slightly. We began to make out the ghostly shapes of other fishing boats, probably French, around us. France was closer than you thought; all you needed was a passport and you could be swilling plonk and munching frites with mayonnaise in no time – 'cept Jack wouldn't touch frites and mayonnaise as long as he lived. To explain why he told a story about a riotous evening in Dieppe with some French fishermen, terminated in spectacularly horrible fashion by food poisoning.

Out on deck the dogfish was flapping ever more feebly. The rainbow had gone from its back. I almost felt sorry for it. Wayne brewed up more sweet tea. The wind was picking up, blowing the mist into wispy strands, whipping back our hair, raising the sea so the *John Paul* rode the waves in a mesmerizing rhythm.

The chimney of Shoreham Power Station was visible first, then Hove and Brighton were there to the right, a low grey smudge on the horizon. I was disappointed that, despite the breeze, the mist was refusing to lift properly and give a clear, sharp view. In the hazy conditions only the seafront buildings that were white or cream had sufficient brightness to stand out. The rest merged into an undifferentiated grey background. And as the only buildings, by and large, painted white or cream were Regency or early Victorian, I found myself looking at the Brighton seafront as it would have been in the mid-nineteenth century. The *John Paul* had turned into a time machine.

This perspective from the sea was an interesting one in other ways. The piers, so insistently obtrusive from the shore, were now foreshortened, ugly. You saw mainly the forest of black seaweedy piles holding them up, and if you did not know what they were, had never seen a pier, would wonder at their function. The white frontages shimmering through the haze, from Adelaide Crescent on the left to Lewes Crescent on the right, looked like stage flats, betrayed the original and essential showiness of the thinking behind them. Brighton was like those people who get dolled up to sit at Mediterranean pavement cafés and look out at passers-by, to see and be seen. Brighton stood on the very edge of England, faced the world and said, 'Look at me, aren't I something?'

Lobster were a midnight-blue colour, as beautiful as they were stupid and violent. They had articulated fan tails edged with orange feathers – you imagined Ellen Terry cooling herself off with one. They clicked like Meccano. Their pots were the shape of dog kennels.They wandered in and found it impossible to reverse out. More fish came up with the lobster pots, flashing silver and yellow. Wayne threw them in the tray, on top of the dogfish which was now definitely dead; it had not moved even its gills for a good half-hour.

Or was it? The insult of having tiddlers thrown at it seemed to bring it back to life. It opened its eyes, its gills began to work, it mouthed silent pleas for help. I had to look away.

We were moving west to east, parallel to the shore, about a mile out to sea – Roedean looking, as always, like an asylum; a great undulating frontage of chalk cliffs; St Dunstan's Institute for the Blind, with its long, wide, easily negotiable corridors; windmill, Rottingdean, more cliffs, Peacehaven – sailing from buoy to buoy, emptying and rebaiting the lobster pots. I was becoming obsessed with the dogfish. Every time I assumed it had expired, it produced further signs of life. A good three hours must have passed since it came up in a crab pot. Was this normal?

Wayne set about the dogfish. He picked it up and placed its

head on the side of the boat. He took a gutting knife and made an incision behind the head. The dogfish moved when he cut it; its head waved from side to side like a cobra's. Wayne swore, picked up the dogfish by the tail with both hands and brought its head down with all his strength against the side of the boat. He held it aloft by the tail. The body still moved. He bludgeoned it again, took the knife and sliced off its head. Lying on the deck, the head looked like a rubber toy. A kid might insert his fingers into it from the back and peck a girl's nose with it in class. But it was *still* looking at me with its green eyes. Then Wayne threw the head overboard, for which I was deeply grateful.

As Wayne gutted it, rubbery purple and grey sacs spilled out and shivered like mercury. He had to break off at this point. We had arrived at another buoy and the crew had to empty and rebait another set of lobster pots. Wayne flung the mutilated body of the dogfish back in the tray by my feet. The headless, gutless body lay there, and while I watched it moved! I told myself this was merely the action of nerve endings, insensate electrical impulses. But it didn't help. The dogfish moved again, flapping its tail in what looked like a perfectly measured way.

We had been at sea for eight hours and the dogfish had been out of the water for at least half that time. We dealt with the last of the lobster pots and Jack opened the throttle and headed back towards the Marina. Lee made more tea and Wayne resumed his struggle with the dogfish. He made a nick in the skin at the head end and attempted to peel it back down to the tail. He tugged and pulled and cursed, but the skin would not peel back. 'Would you believe it?' he said. He held up the stump of body, with the skin flayed and bloody at the fat end, and the dogfish remains waved from side to side. He took the knife to the skin and in the end had to peel the fish with the knife as if it were a large, slippery tuber. He was left with a tube of pink flesh with a criss-cross pattern on it which made it look like a length of garden hose.

For the journey back to town from the Marina, I opted to go in the back of the van rather than sit practically in Wayne's lap in the front. I lay among the tubs of crab and lobster, looking at the cloudy sky as we kangarooed and backfired our way back to the fishermen's arches. We detoured north-east initially, to the housing estates of Woodingdean serrating the first curves of downland on the very edge of town. Here Jack had a call to make: the widow of a fisherman he always saw right with a juicy crab or two when he returned from a sea trip.

He came back up the drive wiping his hands on his jeans and said: 'Thissa a rough area, so they say. You'd be rough too if you had nothing.' Fishermen current and retired lived here and in neighbouring Moulsecoomb. A particularly gruesome child murder had happened up here in the eighties – nothing to do with fishing families, but this was what it was like where they lived. It seemed wrong that the workers of such an old-established industry, the lifeblood of old Brighton, should be shunted out here on the edge of things.

A fisherman's wife, who sold fish from the seafront arches, could trace her family back for hundreds of years, to when they lived in the Lanes, where a Mexican restaurant or a condom shop was now. She wore a headscarf, had fine tanned cheeks like delicate deerskin and startling blue eyes. She looked old, not in years (she was barely fifty) but in centuries, epochs. When she went home to her microwave oven and leylandii hedging she looked like a fish out of water.

The tubs I lay among in the back of the truck were covered with squares of tarpaulin. Under one of them was the tray of fish. I lifted the tarpaulins gingerly till I found the one. The dogfish was there, Wayne's supper. Already it had lost its pink sheen and looked dead and white. I left the tarpaulin off and watched it as we drove back on to the seafront road, past

Laurence Olivier's house in Royal Crescent, past Terence Rattigan's on Marine Parade. And finally the dead white tube that was all that was left of the dogfish twitched.

Chapter Four

For once we sat down, finding a table at the back. The light of midday blazed bright as magnesium through the windows in the front, but here in the shadows, next to the passage to the gents, the gloom was ripe for story-telling. The business of Guil Shakfpeare (as Roger wrote it on a beermat) had started with one of Roger's explosive, Toad-like obsessions, which tended rapidly to burn themselves out – in this case, a fascination with swords. Roger was an enthusiastic member of a local amateur dramatic society, which was why he had started looking at pointed weaponry.

The am-dram scene in Brighton was unlike anywhere else. In the damp, Calor-heated tabernacles of Brighton and Hove, you put on plays with former warm-up men for Max Miller, crumbling ex-Tiller girls with bone-crushing handshakes, and bit-part players in some of the lesser *Carry On*s. They knew instinctively how to move in and out of the limelight, how to hurl their voices like encyclopaedias at the far, pointed windows.

Working with them was like playing parks football with ex-pros – not George Best and Denis Law, but honest toilers like, say, Tony Dunne and David Sadler, who played in the same team but whom few remember now. Roger loved it. He had stammered dysfunctional dialogue in Pinter, worn a ridiculous peruke in Molière and twirled a handlebar moustache in Wesker. Now they were thinking of tackling a Shakespeare history or two and Roger's thoughts had turned to swords.

At weekends and lunchtimes he would nose about Brighton's junk and bric à brac shops. He bought his first sword – a heavy ceremonial weapon, perhaps made for Freemasons – and discovered he really liked it. He liked its bluntness because, like a cat's paws, it had the potential for sharpness. He thrilled to the sense of balance between short handle and long blade. But knowing it wasn't real, had never been wielded in anger, he quickly grew dissatisfied with it. He wanted a real sword, one that could conceivably have slashed a Russian's ear in the Crimea. And so he began to hunt, and one day his quest took him to a shop called Balchin's, in a cul de sac fifty yards off Preston Street.

I went there myself after hearing the story, only to find the place padlocked up with a For Sale notice stuck on the plate-glass frontage, cleared out save for a copy of *It Shouldn't Happen to a Vet* lying in the middle of the floor. But Roger caught it in time for it to yield up its secret. He found no swords there, just a bayonet, which may or may not have stuck the Boche at Beaumont Hamel. He was debating with himself whether it was worth the £30 – stubby and brutish compared to the romanticism of swords, but on the other hand it stood a good chance of having seen some real, gut-spurting action – when he backed into a picture propped against a bamboo umbrella stand. He turned round to steady the picture and found himself staring down into a pair of off-centre pupils.

I have only seen the picture since it was professionally restored, yet even in its original, shabby state it must have stopped him in his tracks. There was something about those eyes. Roger put down the bayonet – forgetting about both bladed weapons and amateur dramatics, for ever, as it turned out – hoisted the picture in its wobbly frame and brought it towards the plate-glass window. Through the dusty glass he would have seen the delicately drawn head and shoulders of a bearded man with receding hair, probably in his thirties, with long nose and slightly hooded lids above those strangely configured eyes. The man wore a high bodice-type jacket with big buttons and a wide, floppy collar. Where the tunic faded out towards the bottom of the picture was an inscription. At this point Roger felt a spurt of adrenalin to his heart.

Holding the picture closer and adjusting its angle towards the window, he read the inscription several times so there could be no mistaking it: *Guil Shakfpe[a]re 1597* (the A being obliterated by a tear in the paper). He checked the price on the tag – £20 – asked the woman sitting at the old school desk if she would hold it for him, and ran up to the Western Road to find a cashpoint.

There was something of a coincidence attached to the discovery of Guil Shakspeare, for at the time Roger happened to wander into Balchin's junk shop he was reading a book called *Bard or Fraud?*, a recent product of that minor but prolific academic industry dedicated to the question of Shakespeare's true identity. Even conservative scholarship now acknowledged that there was something fishy about a rather dull grain merchant from Stratford, with no record of formal education and a seeming inability to spell his own name the same way twice, producing an *oeuvre* of genius such as human creativity had never equalled.

Were there, for instance, two William Shakespeares, one in Stratford and another – the actor and playwright – in London, and had they somehow been mixed up after their deaths? Or was Shakespeare, a minor actor, a front-man for the real author of the plays and sonnets which bear his name? Was the true, immortal bard that Elizabethan egghead and political intriguer, Francis Bacon; or the Earl of Oxford, Edward de Vere, known to have been a dramatist (whose case was first championed by one John Looney in 1920); or even playwright Christopher Marlowe (though he was officially dead by the time that all but the earliest of Shakespeare's plays were written)?

Roger was bright-eyed with the intrigue of it. To me, though, the biological fact of who he was was scarcely important along-side the fact of his work. Shakespeare was everyone and no one. Like Brighton, he reduced writers to list-making. To Harold Pinter, for instance, he was 'a malefactor; a lunatic; a deserter; a conscientious objector; . . . a beggar; a road sweeper; a tinker; a hashish-drinker; . . . a traffic policeman; a rowing blue; a rear gunner; a chartered accountant . . .' (Pinter continues in this uncharacteristically incontinent vein for hundreds of words.) On the other hand, if Roger had really found a true likeness of Shakespeare, whoever he may have been, it would be a sensational turn-up.

That day, as he stared at his new acquisition propped to one side of the fireplace in the Sillwood Place flat, Roger picked up *Bard or Fraud?* to remind himself of some salient facts: there were only two likenesses of Shakespeare in existence which could lay any claim to being authentic, i.e. drawn from life. One was the Droeshout engraving, the rather perfunctory, stylized engraving which appears on the First Folio of his works – and on numberless editions since. The second was the so-called Chandos portrait, named after one of its owners, attributed to a John Taylor and reckoned to have been painted in 1610, six years before Shakespeare's death. This shows Shakespeare looking not unlike a balding Anthony Sher, wearing a gold earring in his left ear and a white collar with two drawstrings hanging down over his black tunic. But now suddenly, after four hundred years, here was the possibility of a third.

As the late-afternoon sunlight streamed in through the windows of his flat, Roger allowed himself the luxury of Ariel-like flights of fancy. He imagined the fame that would follow from the discovery and authentication of a hitherto unknown likeness of the greatest writer who ever lived. And, being a cartoonist, saw his own eyes as the windows on a fruit machine, and pound signs clocking up in them so fast they turned into a blur. 'Pure crap, of course,' he said, slurping the last of his first pint, wiping the foam from his lips and grinning.

But not *all* crap. The portrait was not an original, as he had seen when, calming down, he wiped the dust from the glass and examined it closely in the sunlight. But it still looked like an old print. So he had an antiquarian book, map and print seller in the Lanes give it the once-over. He confirmed it as a lithograph, probably from the early nineteenth century, probably not English – and the game was on again. The name and date implied that what he had bought was a copy of an original portrait. To keep Guil Shakspeare alive he had to establish this, or go one better and actually find the original portrait, if indeed it still existed.

He took a transparency of the portrait on a large-format camera and over several weeks did the rounds with it, sometimes in person, sometimes by posting copies of the transparency. Experts from the British Museum, the Shakespeare Birthplace Trust, the Folger Shakespeare Library in Washington DC, the V&A and the Smithsonian Institution in Washington DC were all at a loss. It was confirmed as an early-nineteenth-century lithograph, probably French. But it was in the style of the sixteenth century and it did not figure in any of the voluminous records of forgeries of Shakespeare's image which have been collated down the centuries.

No one had seen anything quite like it before. One chap choked back tears when he studied the transparency under a magnifying glass, holding it towards the stormy autumn sky, the swaying plane trees and scudding clouds, beyond his Bloomsbury window. He had been expecting some crude, ten-a-penny likeness, not this beautiful, sensual rendition. He stood from his desk and wove his way to the window, saying to Roger, 'I'm sorry, I wasn't ready for this. It's too much. It's just how I'd like him to have looked.' But he couldn't say more. No one could be tempted to commit themselves by verifying its status as a print taken from a sixteenth-century original. No one would put their neck on the line.

Roger, however, kept the faith, choosing to perceive this

vessel of expert opinion as half full rather than half empty. Guil Shakfpe[a]re was William Shakespeare until and unless proved otherwise, and somewhere out there was the original, sixteenth-century portrait. In 1597, the date on the print, he would have been thirty-three years old. He had already written *Richard III, A Midsummer Night's Dream, Romeo and Juliet* and *The Merchant of Venice*, and bought the second-biggest house in Stratford. 'He was like Andrew Lloyd Webber,' said Roger, 'with all these shows on all over the place. Minting it in. The plump look was in then, it meant you ate well, had means, so they made him look like a porky balding guy in those famous portraits. But he must have had a picture done of himself as he really was, rangy and enigmatic. *Must* have.'

Roger got the next pints in before continuing, and drank off an inch to further oil the tongue. In Brighton there are narrow lanes between buildings that are called twittens, an old Sussex word which is perhaps a corruption of ''twixt and 'tween'. They can have something of the glamour of secret passageways or magical thresholds: you come upon them unexpectedly, as if a flint wall were moving aside to let you in, and they convey you in a trice to another part of town. (Try, for instance, Pool Passage, which leads from Pool Valley bus station, passes behind a hotel kitchen that smells of cooking fat, turns right-angles by a rusting fire escape, runs alongside a buckled wall and past a nest of wheelie bins, and delivers you abruptly into the light and noise of the Old Steine.) Our conversation, which had been proceeding in a reasonably orderly fashion down a straightish line, now veered most disconcertingly down a narrative twitten.

Roger had a cleaner called Florence who did for him once a week. 'You've probably met her', he said, 'at some stage when you've been down.' And in fact I did remember her, chiefly because Roger had told me she was a grandmother, yet she looked barely older than we were. Over the months, as she introduced order and system to his chaotic flat, they became friends; and presently she felt she knew Roger well enough to comment on the layout of the flat, offering advice on the best place to hang pictures or put tables.

At first this advice was occasional, and diffidently offered, but slowly she grew more insistent. Roger found himself irritated by her presumption, not to mention her strange notions of where to site things. He was, after all, an artist and had strong ideas of how his flat should look, without the hired help sticking her oar in. Matters came to a head when Roger hung some portraits he had done of jazz and blues musicians – Blind Lemon Jefferson was one – for a series of CD covers and Florence told him casually they were on the wrong wall. 'Thanks for the advice, Flo,' he had said, 'but I'm happy with the wall they're on.'

'I'm telling you,' she said, 'you'd feel better if they were on *there*.' And she pointed her vacuum-cleaner nozzle at a blank space on a different wall.

Roger had lost his temper at this point, and decided to spell out some ground rules. Much as he liked her, he said, he paid her to clean the flat, not to redesign it. If he wanted her advice he would ask for it. She responded by making him coffee and telling him a story. Off we dived down another twitten.

As a child Flo had been what Roger described as a space cadet. She invented imaginary friends whom she talked to, often preferring their company to real people. She was dreamy and distracted and was always getting clips round the ear from her stepmother for bringing half-squashed hedgehogs and birds with broken wings into the house. She believed she could heal them, and some, she claimed to Roger, she did make better, but the ones who died she would bury, after elaborate ceremonies in her own, made-up language, in a miniature cemetery she laid out at the bottom of the garden.

At seventeen, after getting married and having a baby, she began to have 'psychic episodes'. The first was at a hairdresser's. She was under a dryer when she received a message about the elderly woman under the dryer next to her. She was to tell the woman not to worry. Her husband was very ill but he wouldn't die. She had no idea where this information came from; she wondered if she was mad; yet the impulse to pass it on was so strong that she couldn't stop herself leaning over, taking the woman by the hand and delivering the message. To her amazement the woman reacted calmly, with gratitude, as if this were a reasonably normal occurrence in her everyday social intercourse. But from that moment Flo understood that she had a sensitivity to degrees of information, intelligence and power beyond the range of most people, and that she could use this sensitivity to do good. 'She even exorcised a ghost that haunted Sillwood Place,' said Roger. 'A sailor. Probably still pining for a servant girl who worked there, Flo reckoned.'

So Roger agreed to hang his pictures where Flo suggested and, although he couldn't say he felt particularly better for it, he didn't feel worse either. He did not think to ask Flo about the Shakespeare portrait. But one day she had come across the box containing the picture and let out a little cry. 'Roger!' She held up the box gingerly between thumb and forefinger. 'What *is* this? It practically electrocuted me!' Roger showed her the picture and told her the story behind it. Flo said she was sure she and some of her like-minded friends would be able to help in finding out more about it – if it really was Shakespeare, if the original still existed, and where it might be found. So Roger had agreed to go along with a paranormal investigation, strictly to complement the ongoing academic researches.

'There you go.' This was as far as the story had got. Roger raised his glass to Guil Shakspeare and space cadets every-where. The picture was at the restorer's at the moment, which was why I couldn't see it there and then, but when he got it back he was going to take it round to Flo's for its first psychic examination. I was welcome to come along. I said I would love to see the portrait, but I was doubtful about Flo and the psychic claptrap. Roger looked taken aback at this. 'You mean you don't believe her?' he asked. 'What about the story of the hairdresser's?' I said she could have made it up, and he looked thoughtful at this, as if the possibility hadn't struck him. 'Well, what the hell,' he said. 'It's all good fun. Let's have another drink.'

Within a week of this session with Roger in the Grosvenor I had run into Fredda in the same place and found my base in Brighton. The week after that, when I was back in London working on the newspaper, Roger rang to say that the portrait was back from the restorer's and he had fixed up to take it round to Flo's. I said I would be there. Though it was still March, we were in the middle of a sunny, unseasonably warm spell. Roger suggested that we meet an hour before the appointment at Flo's so I could see the picture on my own. How about the Meeting Place, the open-air café on the seafront, seeing the weather was so good?

Squared in by orange windbreaks, the Meeting Place enjoyed its own micro-climate of dazzling light and bearable temperatures so that, rain permitting, it was possible to sit at the plastic tables almost all year round, though there were some days, it was true, in January and February, when it was too bitterly cold for even the hardiest of souls.

The kitchen and servery, a listing, battered kiosk, had been transformed by a plywood fascia running around the top in the silhouette of a fabulous oriental skyline – minarets, domes and towers – unknowingly echoing the theme of the aborted Oriental Gardens and Athenaeum nearby. This decorative flourish struck me as highly imaginative and original for a greasy spoon. Then Fredda told me it was a leftover from when the episode of *Lovejoy* had been filmed in and immediately outside her house. The director needed an outdoor seafront café scene but found the original Meeting Place far too scruffy and depressing as it was. So he put his set designers to work with the words: 'Lighten this shithole up.' Up went the dreamy skyline, around went the orange windbreaks, and as the proprietor couldn't be fagged to take them down after filming, a singular venue was born by default.

Usually the orange windbreaks surrounding the seating area did their job, but on some days, so persistent and insidious were the gusts off the sea that they snuck past the barricades and swirled around the tables with the ferocity of a mini-cyclone, blowing sugar lumps clean off the tables, lifting vacant chairs and setting them down again so it looked as if ghostly practical jokers were at work. When this happened the owner would lift one side, or a section of one side, of the windbreaks, thereby releasing the wind as one uncorks a genie's bottle. The effect of this was to reveal, in place of blank orange canvas, sudden, classic vignettes of Brighton – ocean, West Pier, Palace Pier, Grand Hotel, Brunswick Terrace, or the wide promenade disappearing towards Hove where fops had once strolled and rollerskaters now practised fancy manoeuvres.

On the morning I agreed to meet Roger I caught a taxi from the station to Fredda's, dumped my bags and wandered over to the Meeting Place to discover they had removed a windbreak on the northern, landward side. This created a view of Fredda's house, with my three attic windows at the top, and the crumbling, leprous façade of the art deco Embassy Court next to it.

Embassy Court was architectural Brighton's major embarrassment. When it was built in 1935 its smooth horizontal lines and rounded corners were a smartly administered smack in the face to the surrounding classicism. In fact when Brighton got used to it the two seemed to work well together, but there was no doubting who was boss. Art deco was now, and soon the whole of the seafront would look like Embassy Court. It had uniformed doormen, not dumb waiters; the first penthouse apartments in England; and 'Vista-Glass Sun Parlours'. Actor Rex Harrison and comedian Max Miller, the 'cheeky chappie', moved in.

But the modernization of the seafront architecture, mooted

in the thirties and again in the sixties, never happened. Now Brunswick Town looked fresh as meringue while Embassy Court had the air of off-meat. It had decayed to the point of near-dereliction, due to the neglect of absentee landlords. Its concrete was stained and crumbling, the metal window-frames were rusted and old fridges and Baby Bellings were abandoned like thrown dice along the corridors. Its last distinguished tenant, Keith Waterhouse, had left in 1992. Sudanese refugees had been moved in so that landlords could pocket their housing benefit. Their beautiful, watchful caramel faces peered from behind scraps of curtain in ground-floor rooms as you turned the corner of Brunswick Terrace and Little Western Street.

Waterhouse had lived on the ninth floor, with a balcony overlooking the sea. The last straw had been when New Age travellers moved on to Brunswick Lawns, between the sea and the flats, and kept him awake until 4 a.m. for two nights running. I had experience of these gatherings myself. One calm, warm night I had been woken by the sound of drumming and laughter and looking from my attic windows had seen what I imagined a medieval army on the night before a battle might have looked like. The lawns were a wide avenue of grass that ran for more than half a mile into Hove. What could have been the embers of campfires, but were perhaps improvised barbecues, glowed red in the night, sending up plumes of smoke. People had lit candles, which burned steadily in the still air. The dreadlocked, barefoot grunginess of the New Agers looked like the motley of peasants and footsoldiers. Their drumming was like a plea for strength in the battle that would commence with the dawn. So bewitched was I by this scene that I forgot to feel angry at having been woken up.

There was something about Brunswick Lawns. They were the subject of a strange pen, ink and watercolour drawing done in 1851 by Frederick Nash entitled 'Brunswick Lawns by Moonlight'. This showed the wide avenue of grass thronged with strolling adults, children and dogs; the moon was up, shedding an astonishingly bright but cold white light that reflected from the sea and from ladies' bonnets and petticoats – a grand occasion for touching up and pickpocketing, for assignations, contraband, roast chestnuts and gypsy airs.

On this bright, windy morning, as I waited for Roger, the lawns were continuing the tradition of hosting eccentric gatherings. Spaced equally along them, for a distance of fifty yards or so towards Hove, were four groups of men and women all wearing the sort of wholesome casuals sold in Gap or Next, and with black, Lone Ranger-type masks pulled across their faces. Each group held a rope and every so often the shape of the group would change, as its blinded members shuffled awkwardly in their American loafers and box-fresh trainers, from line to circle to tight bunch and back again. Occasionally someone would shout something which I couldn't quite catch, a sort of gung-ho bark. I watched them closely for several minutes but gleaned no idea whatsoever of what they were doing, or who they might be.

A man in hotel porter's livery, holding a mobile phone, admitted with rolling eyes they belonged to him. 'Yep, my mob,' he said in a South Yorkshire accent. 'Staying at t' Grand. Management consultants from' (he mentioned the name of an American company) 'doin' "role playing exercises".' He apostrophized the phrase with magnificent sarcasm. 'First they have to mek a drop zone for parachootists, then an equilateral triangle. Don't ask me why, but I'm not bothered, like. More I stand here, less work I have to do back at t' hotel.'

At this point a barefoot tramp happened by the café, wearing a long, sandy-coloured coat like ironmongers used to wear. 'Whassat?' he said, momentarily shocked out of his daze.

'Management consultants,' said the hotel porter.

'Cobblers,' replied the tramp.

Not realizing that the locals tended to avoid eating at the Meeting Place, feeling hungry and with Roger running late, I ordered a bacon-and-egg roll with my second cup of coffee.

Rather grandiosely, a loudspeaker announcement told me when it was ready: 'Bacon egg roll please baconegg please thank you.' Was I imagining it or did people regard me with amused amazement as I strolled, with as much insouciance as I could muster, to the kiosk to pick up my breakfast?

The fried egg flapped from the sides of the roll, looking like a joke egg made of moulded plastic. Assuming the yolk was solid, I savaged the roll with my first, ravenous bite. A hot yellow stream spattered over my cheek and neck. I was trying to clear up the mess with a thin, non-absorbent paper napkin when Roger arrived clutching a large flat cardboard box and apologizing for being late. 'And what the hell's going on there?' he asked, jerking his thumb at the Lone Rangers on Brunswick Lawns.

I was keen to get my hands on the picture, but seeing the state of those hands Roger instructed me to go and wash them in the sea first. I crunched down the pebbles in front of the café to the shoreline, knelt and bathed my hands in the foam, just where the green sea turned to white, then held them up into the wind to dry as I jogged back to the terrace.

'Pass the salt,' said Roger, 'and the ketchup, and the vinegar.' He drew the picture from its box and used the cruets to anchor its edges against the white plastic table. 'There.' He sat back grinning and looked at me for my reaction.

I wasn't sure what I had been expecting – perhaps a rounder face, more like the vague notion of Shakespeare we carry around in our heads, based on old textbooks, which of course in turn would have been based on the two most famous portraits Roger had already told me about. But, as he pointed out, that is a closed circle of thought. Or perhaps I was expecting or hoping for some inspirational flash of certitude, some communication, down the centuries, from the portrait itself.

The fact that it had been so well restored perhaps detracted from its mystique. The tears in the paper had been patched up so they were scarcely visible; it just didn't look that old. I had to admit though, the portrait itself was a work of great delicacy and skill. Whoever he may have been, the sitter was a man of refinement, of both action – as evidenced by his bony nose and strong chin – and reflection – witness those bewitching off-centre pupils within oval irises. Each silken hair on his pate had been lovingly rendered. Light reflected strongly from his head as if he might have been out of doors or in a tall, airy studio. Roger could see me struggling to hide my disappointment, nevertheless.

'You don't like it,' he said flatly.

'Of course I *like* it,' I said. 'It's fantastic. It's just that—'

'You think it doesn't look like Shakespeare.'

'Well, it wasn't quite what I was expecting.'

'You've been brainwashed,' he said. 'That's why. You've got to clear your head of any preconceptions of what Shakespeare looked like. Then you can start to see Shakespeare coming through.'

'Are you sensitives, either of you?' asked the man with the grey hair and long fingers. Flo had introduced him as Larry, one of Brighton's most respected mediums. When he looked from Roger to me and back again, I fancied for a split second he could read our thoughts, and felt myself mentally apologizing for my scepticism just in case.

We said no, assuming he had been asking whether we had psychic powers, but did that mean, then, that we were *in*sensitives? I felt indignant at the notion. I may not have been on intimate terms with the spirit world, but I wasn't brute blood and muscle either. Our answer put us in the minority among the six of us present. We were the defectives. If mediumship was like being a satellite dish, picking up messages from the Other Side, as Larry proceeded to suggest, making the analogy with sweeps of his arm and a self-satisfied smile on his lips, Roger and I were a couple of tin cans joined by a string.

Six of us sat in Flo's sitting room in Hove while her dog, banished to the garden for the duration, hovered outside the window looking sorry for himself. The sound of tribal drums floated softly from the CD player. Lumps of polished purple quartz lay in front of the fireplace. Flo fussed around with plates of biscuits and cups of herbal tea. Her friend Jackie, sitting next to me on one sofa, said she had come to mediumship late and was still very much at the learning stage. She could pick up a lot from the likes of Larry, a practitioner for some thirty-five years, and his colleague Doreen. Doreen, sitting alongside Larry, nodded and smiled. She was stout and perspired slightly on the upper lip.

They were in no hurry to commence the business at hand, the reason they were all here, which was to look at the Shakespeare portrait and, if they could, give us more information on it. Instead I fancied they were enjoying the novelty of being the dominant social group, nattering casually about 'Spirit' and 'coming through', 'higher planes' and 'passing over'.

Larry asked if he could borrow Roger's wristwatch. He rubbed the watch as if assessing the quality of a piece of fabric, he raised his eyebrows and cocked his head and, on the strength of the vibrations he had received from the watch, proceeded to give a reading of Roger's character. He said Roger was considered to be an extrovert, happy-go-lucky sort of chap, but inside he was a mess. His problem was that he was afraid not of failure, but of success. He was talented and driven, but he was fearful of going that extra half-yard that might make all the difference. What Roger needed – in Larry's opinion, and pardon his French – was a good kick up the arse.

Roger took this in pretty good part, I thought, nodding slowly in agreement and smiling ruefully. Larry handed back the watch and looked pleased with himself. 'And now you, my dear, if you don't mind.' He pointed to Jackie's bracelet. I passed it between them. Larry dangled the bracelet from his long, shiny, rather fishy fingers. 'I get a lot of sadness,' he said.

76

Jackie shook her head, furrowed her brow. 'Not really,' she said.

'You wouldn't say you've had a sad life?'

'Not so far,' she said. 'In fact I've been very happy, I would say, all in all.'

'Of course,' said Larry, 'I could be talking about a previous owner of the bracelet. Previous owners come through just as strongly sometimes. It's an old bracelet, isn't it?'

'It was my grandmother's,' said Jackie.

'Ah, that must be it.' He rubbed the bracelet and looked puzzled. 'Do you have children?'

'*You* tell *me*,' said Jackie.

A fuse seemed to blow in Larry's head at this. 'Right!' he said. His eyes blazed with anger. 'That's enough.' He handed me the bracelet to give back to Jackie. 'You know what you've done? You've closed the door. I've been doing this for forty years. I don't need to prove myself.'

An uncomfortable silence settled on the gathering, filled by drums and wailing from the loudspeakers. Flo asked if anyone wanted more tea. We shook our heads. Still agitated, Larry scratched his neck and breathed deeply. Roger spoke. 'Well, I think at this point . . .' He leaned over the side of his chair and picked up the cardboard box containing the portrait. He laid it on the coffee table in front of Larry and Doreen. They hunched forward and stared intently at it.

Larry said, 'May I?' and lifted it up, weighing it gingerly. 'There's certainly something coming off of it.' He handed it to Doreen and raised his eyebrows at her.

Doreen took it, closed her eyes and went very still for a few seconds. 'Mmm,' she said at last. She put the portrait back on the table.

'Want to have a go, Jackie?' asked Flo. Flo herself wouldn't take part, she had told us. Jackie, still smarting from Larry's outburst, looked doubtful. 'Come on,' cajoled Flo. 'It's not a competition. Just relax.'

Flo handed Jackie the picture. She stared at it and closed her eyes, opened them again and stared at the ceiling then back at the portrait, and finally shook her head and said, ''Fraid not, nothing. Sorry.'

'Don't *apologize*,' said Flo.

It was down to Larry and Doreen. Larry took the portrait back and said, 'I've got to confess, I've been told people have thought it may be of Bill Shakespeare, and I can't help seeing his name written here. I have to say I don't. But that's not to say it isn't interesting in its own right. I can certainly feel something there . . .' He laid the flat of his hand on the portrait and screwed up his eyes with concentration, then shook his head. 'It's not coming through clearly enough, I'm afraid. And now, if you'll excuse me a minute, ladies and gentlemen, I'm nipping outside for a cigarette.'

Larry disappeared through the kitchen and appeared a moment later in the garden beyond the living-room window, where he patted the dog and smiled nervously as he smoked, unsure how well we could see him, or whether we were watching him at all.

'Well, I think I'm going to have to agree with Larry about the Shakespeare,' said Doreen when he was out of the room. 'I don't know why, I'm thinking of Milan. I'm picking up a doctor . . . no, is it a doctor or is it somebody even more learned . . . a doctor of philosophy perhaps.' She closed her eyes and we expected more, but she said, 'Milan, philosophy, that's all I'm getting.'

When Larry returned he said, 'Let's have another go.' He narrowed his eyes. 'I'm drawn to Holland. A Dutch painter.'

'Oh really?' said Doreen. 'I thought more Milan.'

'Milan?' He assessed this new information. 'It could be a Milanese artist working in Holland.'

'Or', said Doreen, 'a Dutch artist working in Milan.'

'True,' he said, but his heart wasn't in it and at this point the session fell flat. The atmosphere had been a bit tense since the spat between Jackie and Larry, so perhaps it wasn't surprising that Roger's mysterious picture had failed to excite the company's imagination. Roger talked about the portrait from an art-historical point of view, the fact that it bore the characteristics of a foreign rather than domestic style – so in that sense, either Holland or Milan might be bang on. But he failed to enthuse. Flo again offered to make more tea, which everyone politely declined. And then, on the spur of the moment, with the afternoon drifting to an unsatisfactory conclusion, I had an idea.

I rummaged in my shoulder bag, produced the postcard of the painting *Breakfast in Brighton* and handed it to Larry. 'I don't suppose', I said, 'you could tell me where the original of that painting is, currently?'

Chapter Five

Edward le Bas's painting had developed into something of an obsession since I had first set eyes on the postcard. The previous week I had popped into the Brighton Museum and Art Gallery, expecting to find the painting there, hanging high in one of the former Pavilion stables, nodded over by a uniformed attendant resting her varicose legs. I always knew the painting would be big somehow, though the dimensions weren't given on the postcard.

I imagined it big enough to feel as if you might step into it, into that sunlit breakfast room, tip an imaginary hat to the two ladies, as one would have been expected to do in 1950, say, 'Grand morning, ladies,' and 'Morning, Polly,' to the parrot, then fling up the sash windows and fly off into the background, over the garden fence, the park on the other side of the road, the domes and towers, over the glittering aquamarine sea, beyond the horizon, off the edge.

Postcards of the painting – the same as the card that had been sent to the newspaper office – were on sale in the foyer of the Museum and Art Gallery. I bought half a dozen and asked in which room I might find the original. It wasn't owned by the gallery, the chap behind the desk told me, it was in a private collection. However, the owner had lent the painting for an exhibition here in 1995 – he produced the catalogue from that exhibition – and the Keeper of Fine Art was the person to talk to if I wanted further information.

I called the Art Gallery and spoke to a woman who explained that they had a policy, for obvious reasons, of not giving out details of private collectors, but if I cared to write a letter and send it to her she would forward it to the owner of *Breakfast in Brighton*. The letter I wrote – explaining my motives in wishing to see and understand more of the painting – was necessarily personal, so it was strange to have no idea of the person who would receive and read it. Would sun slant across my letter, when it was first read, and how hot would that sun be? Would the person at the breakfast table be a porn baron, with tigerskin sofas, or an heiress with a doge's commode? I licked the envelope and posted it into oblivion.

That had been a few days before and I had not yet had a reply. Now, in Flo's sitting room in Hove, I thought I would play a little game with touchy, fishy-fingered Larry. He didn't bat an eyelid when I asked him where he thought the original painting was. He fired his answer straight back: 'I'm getting St Albans. I don't know why.'

While I awaited a reply to my letter from the owner of the painting I decided to start from the beginning. According to the museum catalogue, *Breakfast in Brighton* showed a breakfast scene in a ground-floor room of Clifton Terrace, looking out under the canopied window, over the gardens on the far side of the road, as far as the copper spire of the Metropole Hotel and the ocean beyond.

Clifton Terrace, near the brow of a hill which climbs towards the Downs, was a cracking little street, the perfect address for an ageing but still sexy concert pianist played by, say, Francesca Annis in a television murder mystery. Its white-stuccoed, semi-detached villas were built on the cusp between Georgian curves and Victorian rectitude. What really set it off were the little canopies, like bonnets, which shielded the bay windows, dangling pointed wooden slats known as dags or dagging which you also get on Victorian railway stations.

On a warm spring morning, such as Edward le Bas might have been striving to show in his painting, I puffed up the steep hill from the Western Road to find that little had changed in nearly fifty years. In the distance, the Metropole had lost its green copper tower – in *Brighton Rock* this is described as looking 'like a dug-up coin verdigrised with age-old mould' – and a large block of flats called Sussex Heights had been built directly behind it; the trees in the little park across the road had grown tall, blocking some light; but the houses were there, the canopies and the dagging, and their glorious sea views which would no doubt feature extensively in scenes of Francesca Annis practising her scales in my imaginary murder mystery.

Outside number 6 or 7 a man was up a stepladder. The canopy above the window of his front room had been removed from its frame.The man held some dagging in place against the underside of the frame and leaned back to judge the effect. Apparently satisfied, he slowly descended the ladder and was about to go inside, still holding the piece of dagging, when I called him. 'Excuse me. I was wondering . . .' I stood at the gate feeling like the emissary of a religious cult, or a bogus roofing contractor. 'Are you familiar with this painting?'

I leaned over his gate and held up the postcard. As he came up he placed the piece of dagging in the top pocket of his shirt so it looked like a particularly well starched handkerchief. 'Ah yes, ye-e-e-s,' he said, put at ease by the sight of the painting. 'It was painted, I believe, from number ten. Slightly before our time here, but I remember being told about it. See, the canopy is still there, and the railings around the bottom of the window.' The location of the fireplace in the painting, on the left as you looked out of the window, was also significant, he said, as all even-numbered houses had their fireplaces in this position. 'The artist chappie', he went on, 'lived in a house at the back, so I believe, in Vine Place. Connie Hook lived there then, I think that's supposed to be her with the silver hair. I don't know who the other woman was.'

It was unaccountably exciting to discover the name of the silver-haired lady. Connie Hook! Back in the street, I looked at the card. Connie wore a red jacket or cardigan, but the other woman was bare-armed. So either it was a touch chilly that morning, despite the brightness, and the dark-haired woman was a hardy soul, or Connie Hook had been a sensitive sort, an orchid.

Emboldened by my progress, I now went up to the door of number 10 and knocked. As I waited for someone to come to the door I studied the dagging at the top of the window and the wrought-iron railings at the bottom and compared them with the painting. The very same! I stood on tiptoe trying to see inside the front room. There was, at least, no birdcage in the bay window, no parrot. After several minutes, when I was about to give up and go, a woman came to the door, an American.

She had presumably just washed her hair for she had twisted a towel up into a turban on her head. She said she knew nothing about the painting. I told her it had almost certainly been painted in her front room. I tried to get her to look properly at the evidence, the card, but she didn't seem interested. 'Go see Mr' – she mentioned the name and house number of the man I had just spoken to and shut the door.

I spent the next two weeks waiting impatiently for a reply to the letter I had sent to the unknown owner of *Breakfast in Brighton*. And while I waited I verified the existence of Connie Hook, or at least of the name Hook. According to successive editions of *Kelly's Brighton Directory*, which listed the owner-occupier of every house and flat in every street in Brighton, No.10 Clifton Terrace had been the property of Hook, Wltr. Chas., from the late 1940s until the early 1960s. Walter and Constance Hook. Wally and Connie. It had a ring to it.

Finally a letter arrived. The envelope was of heavy, expensive paper, the handwriting unfamiliar but stylish, in black ink, real ink. This must be it. Unable to read the postmark, I tore at the envelope. Could it be from St Albans? What would I do if it was? But the address on the letterhead was a village in Norfolk, which left me feeling obscurely relieved.

The address, Something Hall, sounded grand, the paper was thick and expensive, the letter had been professionally word-processed and signed by a man: James Warren. 'Thank you for your letter with reference to Breakfast in Brighton. I would be delighted for you to come and see the painting which is hanging in Norfolk at the above address . . .' I telephoned Mr Warren's secretary to make an appointment.

Mr Warren's secretary had warned me on the telephone about the automatic gates. They were tall, wrought-iron, between modern brick gateposts. 'Drive up to within two feet of them and they will open automatically. Sounds sinister, I know, but you can't be too careful these days.' I nosed up to the gates, which began to open – silent and, sure enough, sinister. I drove up a drive to a gravel forecourt.

A heavily suntanned woman ran alongside my car as I was parking and said peremptorily, 'Are you the photographer? You're fifty minutes late.' I said I wasn't and I explained my business. 'My apologies,' she said. 'We're expecting a photographer and a reporter from one of the glossies. The reporter's turned up but where is the damned camera chappie? Everything is running late because of him. I'll tell my husband you're here.'

Presently Mr James Warren came crunching across the forecourt gravel, hand outstretched. He was tall and thin, pin-striped, handsome, also suntanned. 'Sorry about the mix-up,' he said. 'Pleased to meet you. Warren.' I asked him what interest the glossy magazine had in him. He was cheerily evasive, waving his arm and saying, 'Oh, you know, one has interests and concerns which other people may find . . .' he searched for the right word, 'illuminating.'

Mr Warren took me into his house, which was a Victorian

mansion, as deep as it was wide, packed snugly with tall-ceilinged rooms, laced with dark corridors. The vertical planes were crowded with paintings. He said he was taking me directly to see a certain painting. The others passed in a blur as I followed him, trying to keep up with his long strides down the long gloomy corridors. He kept up a running commentary as he went: 'That's a Sickert, a Utrillo there, Pissarro, Augustus John, Duncan Grant of course, I'm particularly fond of that . . .'

At one point we scooted through a sort of half-room, where the corridor widened for a few feet or so. There was enough space for an *escritoire* with chairs on either side, and sitting in these chairs were two figures. They made me jump when I saw them; then I thought they might be dummies, but they were real enough. One was a woman, head down, who scribbled furiously in a notebook – the magazine reporter, presumably. The other was a man in a bow-tie who leaned back in his chair with his hands knitted behind his head. 'And you say that was in 1975?' said the woman as we passed. Warren failed to acknowledge these people in the slightest way, as if they were apparitions and only I had seen them.

Only once did he pause, by a glass display case. 'If you like beautiful things,' he said, 'this will move you. A miniature silver dinner service presented to the Comte de Paris by the Burghers of Paris in 1861. Observe the exquisite detail.' The plates were a thumbnail's width, the cut-glass port bottles had their own stoppers, the candlesticks their own wax candles, scarcely thicker than thread. As I looked, Warren set off again down the corridor and I had to break into a jog to catch up.

I assumed, naturally enough, that the particular painting he was about to show me was *Breakfast in Brighton*. Though perfectly friendly, Warren struck me as a man permanently in a hurry. I would be lucky to have more than ten minutes with him at this rate, and there was only so much I could find out in such a short time. Even before I had seen the painting I began to feel disappointed.

He led me into a huge drawing room with windows the size of a cinema screen looking over a lake. A fountain in the middle of the lake jetted fifty feet into the air, making it look like a miniature Lake Geneva. Portraits of Victorian patresfamilias lined the wall opposite the windows. He steered me round the marble fireplace, on top of which stood an ornate ormolu clock, and indicated a smallish picture hanging on the recessed wall beyond. It was a portrait of a man standing by an easel, holding a paintbrush and palette. Behind him light flooded through the corner of a window. The man was thin, straight-backed and tallish. He had a trimmed beard and looked like a symmetrical D. H Lawrence. 'My relative Edward le Bas, the chap who painted *Breakfast in Brighton*,' said Mr Warren. 'Self-portrait, looking frightfully serious. He looked more ebullient as he got older.' And then Mr Warren told me a story.

Edward was in his beautiful studio in Glebe Place, Chelsea, designed by Charles Rennie Mackintosh, one of the most uplifting private spaces in London. The rooms were tall, the windows floor-to-ceiling. Around the walls were hung many of the paintings which now adorned the rooms and corridors of Mr Warren's house. More paintings were stacked against the furniture, the chaise longue, the armchairs, the numerous easels. It was an unusual space in being both for work and for pleasure. There were rather tatty old kilims scattered over the wooden floorboards. There was a drinks cabinet and a gramophone. There were tables on which were silver cigarette cases, always kept stocked, and boxes of cigars. The paraffin heaters lent it a petroly air in winter; in summer there were bowls of fruit – bananas, peaches and lemons, still scarce and prized in those post-war days. And there was the light, falling in glorious, stilly cascades through those huge windows, making him think of painting – doing it and looking at it – as frequently as men are now said to think about sex.

That said, Edward le Bas was, as Mr Warren put it, frightfully idle when it came to doing his own painting. A corner of the studio was always cleared for the purpose. Here the floor-boards were spattered with paint, the cupboards bore a pleasing patina of pigmentation. Tubes of colour lay about, a picture in progress was always propped on an easel. But Edward was easily distracted. With paintbrush loaded and poised over a canvas, he would start thinking of his latest acquisition, for he had inherited a vast sum of money and collected paintings freely.

He would decide to have another quick gaze at his latest painting and so he would smear the paint on his brush back on to the palette, wipe his hands on his smock and step over to where he had propped it. Pulling it from a stack of others – he would take months, if not years, to hang new acquisitions – he would carry it over into the strongest of the light and stand there transfixed with pleasure, smoking, gazing, shaking his head in admiration, forgetting entirely about his own work. If Edward had been less modest, more driven, less rich and more hungry perhaps, he might well have achieved fame as an artist. But his own work was always more tiresome than other people's; other people did other people's work, but only he could do his own, and though the finished product gave him much pleasure – the moment when he dropped E.L.B. into the bottom right-hand corner being particularly sharp – the doing it was often a bind.

He was also too much of a host for his own good, not enough of a guest. Successful, driven artists don't throw their own parties; they turn up briefly, tantalizingly, at other people's. But Edward loved having people round to the Chelsea studio – from a sozzled paintsmith at ten in the morning to an evening's worth of minor royalty. The latter sort of visit entailed the hire of a couple of Mrs Mops to efface the more grotesque hygienic abominations of bohemian bachelorhood, though he always left a lobster in the bath. In the former case, he might actually remove some half-full spirits bottles from the drinks cupboard and put them on the table, to imply a previous night's debauch, before his visitor reached the top of the stairs from the front door. It was about making people feel at home.

On this particular morning he hovered somewhere between these two extremes. The place needed a bit of a dust – nothing he couldn't manage himself – the ashtrays needed emptying and he had ordered a large spray of cut flowers, but that, he thought, would probably do the trick. His guest, due at noon, was a Mrs Dreyfus, New York socialite and avid if indiscriminate collector of twentieth-century art. He had met her the previous month at a weekend party in the Hamptons to which he had been invited by a Manhattan gallery owner he had rather taken a shine to.

'Edward,' said the gallery owner, whose name was Mort, to the assembled partygoers at his beachfront house. '*Ed*ward, where *are* you?' Mort found him on the wooden verandah of the clapboard house, using his hand as a visor as he gazed over the ocean and the distant ships that lay apparently becalmed on the blue haze. 'Ah, there you are. Meet my dear friend and patron, Mrs Dreyfus. Mrs Dreyfus *collects*, Edward . . .'

As the shadows lengthened on the verandah, Mrs Dreyfus had put on a pyrotechnic display of philistinism and egotism that left the seagulls screeching in admiration and Edward simply speechless. In the course of this performance it seemed she had invited herself to Edward's studio when she was next in London, though by that stage he had given up listening to the individual words, as one might cease counting the raindrops of an incipient storm, and was admiring the overall effect – the turban and bangles, the fingernails, the stupidity and the voice like a buzz-saw.

So here he was, about to entertain a visitor who made his rather fastidious flesh crawl. Typical Edward, then, to be too nice to have suggested she took the quick route back to Manhattan, via Long Island Sound, and find himself lumbered with a horror for a guest – except that on this occasion, against all odds and expectations it has to be said, the meeting was to turn to Edward's advantage.

He had recently bought, for a great deal of money at a Paris auction house, a painting by Pierre Bonnard called *Le Bol de Lait*, or *The Bowl of Milk*. It showed a young woman in a long dress, a nightgown perhaps, standing next to a table beneath an open window, through which the morning sun shone brightly. Beyond the window was a carved stone balcony and beyond that the blue sea, glittering in the morning sun. The woman held a wooden ladle and her eyes appeared to be closed as if she were in a trance, or perhaps hadn't woken up properly. On the table, as well as a jug and plate, was a bowl of milk. Next to this table, which was rectangular, was a small circular table on which stood a vase of red flowers. Waiting for Mrs Dreyfus, Edward raised his eyebrows at the Bonnard and sighed.

The doorbell clanged promptly at noon. Mrs Dreyfus filled the door, seemed an affront to the discreet affluence of the street outside. The dress was white, the hair, liberated from the turban, was lacquered into a black helmet. Edward's heart sank even as he said, 'Mrs Dreyfus, what a pleasure to see you again.' Mrs Dreyfus did not like the spiral staircase, which she called 'a medieval elevator or what?'. She felt chilly in the studio, despite the fine spring weather, but looked horrified by the moth-eaten blanket he produced for her shoulders.

Would she care for a drink? She took a highball and as she stepped round the studio, sipping and looking she fell, for once, silent. Then she began to speak. 'I have one of those,' she said, 'and a bigger one of those. I sold off one of *those* just last year . . .' But she spoke uncharacteristically softly; she was whistling in the dark, trying to keep up her spirits, for she had finally met a private collection which, in quality if not quantity, far exceeded her own.

Finally she sat down, looking critically at the drink she still held as she did so, and it was then that she saw the Bonnard, which she had somehow missed in her initial inspection. 'Oh my God,' she said. 'A Bone-arde.' Now she was like a bullying dog who has met his match and changes his tactics, rolling on his belly, licking and fawning over his superior. Edward was wonderful, the studio was sublime, I'm telling you, his collection was unbelievable, the Bone-arde outta this world. She couldn't sit still, she was up and pacing, shoving her nose in the paintings, sniffing the paint, rolling her eyes and making little mewing sounds of ecstasy. And Edward watched this performance in equal degrees of amusement and bafflement. At least, he had to admit, the visit was turning out to be much more interesting than he had expected.

And then she spotted *Breakfast in Brighton*, a coloured chalk drawing Edward had knocked off four years earlier. The strange thing was, as Edward repeated over and over again later when relating the strange story of Mrs Dreyfus, the little chalk drawing was a trifling thing, of virtually no consequence. It had remained stacked and hidden for nearly all of the four years since he had done it, and he had only hung it by chance a few weeks before when looking for a picture of a precise size to replace one he had sold.

Still, she wasn't to be put off. 'Now *this*,' she said. 'Who did *this* now?'

'Oh, that,' said Edward. 'That's a mere . . . an inconsequential daub. I should really take it down.'

'Aren't we being rather British now, Edward?' She pouted alarmingly in his face. 'Are those the initials E.L.B. I see in the bottom right hand corner, by any chance?'

Much to Edward's frustration and embarrassment, Mrs Dreyfus went overboard about this picture he had knocked off in a matter of a few hours, on a duty visit to a relative who lived near him on the south coast. It showed two women at the breakfast table and, as much as anything, had been an exercise in light, the way the morning light fell through the window. But then Mrs Dreyfus astonished him by picking up on this, saying how well he had captured the elusive, vanishing quality of light.

Not only that, she drew a comparison with the Bonnard, the way the glittering sea light fell on the table. She walked from one to the other across the studio, and back again. She held out her arms and marvelled at both simultaneously as if, ridiculously, there was scarcely a cigarette paper's width between them in terms of merit. Quite ridiculous, the woman was obviously barking mad. And yet, in spite of himself, Edward felt flattered, flattered enough to amend his opinion of Mrs Dreyfus. Yes, of course she was vulgar and embarrassing, but she was American after all. When you got to know her a bit, you realized that beneath that philistine exterior beat a heart of some sophistication and discernment. And then, when he was weak, when he was *hers*, she made her suggestion.

Clapping her hands together as she danced between one and the other picture, she declared, 'I have it. I have the solution, Edward. You're gonna love this. What will happen is, you will paint *this* picture' – she tripped on sturdy calves to the chalk drawing – 'in the style of *this* picture' – and she danced back to the Bonnard. 'See?'

Edward laughed and shook his head and scratched his scalp, poured a drink twice as stiff as the first.

'And it's gonna be big, I mean *big*. American big. I wanna feel that light, I wanna be blinded by that light. You're a Bone-arde, baby, but you don't *cost* Bone-arde, now, do you?'

Mr Warren led me back along the passageways of his warren-like house. Where the corridor widened and I had seen the magazine reporter and the man with the bow-tie, there was nobody. The green leather top of the *escritoire* was free of notebooks and clutter, the nap of the velvet chairs on either side was smooth. It reminded me of the house in Hitchcock's *North by Northwest* in which Cary Grant is held down and has whisky poured down his throat before being set loose on a switchback

91

road in his car. When he returns next day with the police, all evidence of the previous night's dirty work has been effaced.

There was, indeed, something seductively fictive about this whole set-up, to do with the casual evidence of immense wealth all around us – the scale of the house, the way our footsteps echoed, the austere, museum-like light falling through the windows on to this abundance of original art by some of the century's greatest painters.

The light was the key to *Breakfast in Brighton*. Mr Warren brought me back to the centre of the house, a vast hallway dominated by an ebony elephant not that much less than life-size and draped with a tiger skin, the tiger's chin resting on its back. On the walls were views of waterways and *peniches*, poplars and picnickers, which Mr Warren confirmed were the work of several famous French Impressionists.

Light flooded the hall from tall windows on the half-landing. The staircase was wide enough for a tightrope walker to proceed upward holding his pole; the steps, cushioned in carpet of a luxuriously deep pile, were so shallow as to make walking seem like gliding. Mr Warren led me past the tall windows and up on to the landing, and nodded back at the wall on the staircase side. The ceiling here was extremely high. The light from the tall windows flooded down, into the hallway, but there was plenty left over to wash through the landing, turning it into a cube of brightness. The light fell on the large painting on the wall on the staircase side, fell on to *Breakfast in Brighton*.

The landing railings turned the space into a viewing gallery. It was big, the painting – about five feet deep by nearly six feet wide – as I had felt, though not known, it would be. The landing was not wide enough to step back and view it as one would wish. Yet the effect of this was to project one forward, towards the painting, as if the railing was all that stopped you from crashing into the breakfast table, from grabbing the edge of the tablecloth for support and bringing the whole lot – the coffee-pot, the teapot, the milk jug, bowl of fruit, jar of marmalade, dish of butter, cups, saucers, plates and knives – crashing down into the hallway, on to the ebony elephant. And Connie Hook, the silver-haired lady, would say, 'Now look what you've done!'

The only thing to do in this circumstance would be to escape – where else but through the window, over the gardens, over the green copper dome of the Metropole, over the sea to France? This had been my fantasy when I first saw the postcard of the painting. Swaying against the railings I relived it now, that much more vividly for the painting being real, in front of me, being big and textured and impossibly brightly coloured – the red of Connie's jacket, the turquoise of the sea. The Japanese porcelain cups, thin and translucent as baby frogs, were exquisitely rendered so you saw the light coming through; the marmalade at the top of the jar glistened. You saw Bonnard's influence, especially in the way a band of shadow lay across a corner of highly polished table not covered by the cloth – just like in *Le Bol de Lait*, the painting spotted by Mrs Dreyfus in Edward's Chelsea studio and now hanging in the Tate Gallery, to which he bequeathed it. Pointing at the fragile translucence of the cups, Mr Warren whispered, 'It's incredible, the way he has caught the light.'

Mr Warren took me to his bedroom. The huge bed was high as a horse. Shoes inhabited by shoe trees were arrayed in highly polished pairs. Outside, beyond the deep sash windows, I saw the top of the fountain, looking like plumes surmounting a ceremonial headdress. Mr Warren indicated a picture hanging in a recess, above the thick sill of one of the windows. '*Breakfast in Brighton*, the prototype,' he said.

It was a small picture, the size of a large sketchpad, executed freely in coloured chalks. Where the light fell most intensely, on the corner of the table, on Connie's silvery mannish hair, Edward had left the paper blank, as would a watercolourist. This sketch was what Mrs Dreyfus had seen and fallen for in Edward's Chelsea studio in 1950.

I hadn't known of the existence of this original *Breakfast in Brighton* until Mr Warren told me the story of Mrs Dreyfus. It affected matters because it had been done quite a bit earlier. When I said to Mr Warren, with the air of a conspirator, that I'd discovered the name of the silver-haired lady, that she was called Connie Hook and had lived at 10 Clifton Terrace with her husband, Walter Charles Hook, at the time *Breakfast in Brighton* was painted, he looked doubtful. For the crucial date was not that of the painting, but of the chalk sketch.

The sketch had been done sometime after the end of the war, and records did not exist for who lived where at that time. *Kelly's Brighton Directory* was not published during wartime nor for some years afterwards. It was a mad, bad time. Houses were bombed, people were killed, men were away, women had desperate affairs, streets were blacked out and nameless. No one knew who was where, who was where they should be, and who wasn't. It is said that John Christie, of 10 Rillington Place infamy, would have been caught much sooner if he hadn't been bumping women off in wartime.

No, as far as Mr Warren knew the silver-haired lady wasn't Connie Hook, of whom he had never heard, but the sister of Edward's lover. Edward's lover had been a half-Japanese concert pianist called Miyadera Schwabe. Though Miyadera was married, to a man named Unwin, she and Edward had a ten-year affair which ended in 1930, when she died in his arms of an unspecified illness. Miyadera had a half-sister called Nellie, who was rather simple and helpless, and Edward had pledged to provide for her and look after her in the event of Miyadera's death. He kept his promise, installing Nellie in 10 Clifton Terrace while he lived off the little alleyway behind, at 3 Vine Place. Because he was a restless soul and travelled a great deal, abroad and between his various houses in England, Edward bequeathed Nellie his beloved parrot, Polly, who features in the painting, and hired a housekeeper, the dark-haired, big-hipped figure in the painting, holding her cup poised, whom Mr Warren remembered as 'substantial and frightening'.

I took a final, lingering look at *Breakfast in Brighton*, then Mr Warren walked me to my car. 'I'm afraid he burned the candle at both ends,' said Mr Warren of Edward. 'Drove an open-topped Bentley, drank the finest wines, smoked like a chimney. He would leave our house in Sussex on a Sunday afternoon, having drunk far too much claret and Taylor's port, and drive back to Brighton. He said he always drove with one wheel in the gutter so he would know immediately if he hit the kerb.'

Chapter Six

The Palace Pier was pulsating, on this Saturday night, about to split open with life. The lightbulbs decorating its superstructure flashed on and off in sequence, giving the impression of flowing light, veins of light flowing through the musculature of the pier. The boardwalk thrummed with feet and the air smelled of virgins and engine oil, of American mustard and Marlboros and dandruff shampoo.

I had arranged to meet friends for a drink at the Offshore Karaoke Bar near the end of the pier. 'Don't worry,' they said. 'It's an absolute shithole. Full of lardy Crawley girls with Michelin midriffs. We'll have a couple of drinks and laugh at them. Then we'll go to a proper bar.' Drinking on the pier on a Saturday night was to be an ironic experience, in which we could laugh at our culture as it used to be fifty or sixty years ago, at the time of *Brighton Rock*. Oh, how simple and unsophisticated were our desires, back then; how semi-literate our palates with their cravings for batter and sugar.

But the irony was a front really. If you were English, you never ceased being unsophisticated because deep down your needs were simple – get out of England! When I stood on piers I thought of my childhood, of the fair that came to Doncaster racecourse for St Leger week – the G-force of the waltzers, the five-legged sheep, the Most Beautiful Woman in the World, the goldfish I had won on a sideshow, which I took back and replaced the following day because the fish wasn't gold enough.

Fairs and piers were a blizzard in your brain, blanking out England for a few precious minutes.

The karaoke bar was crammed with kids drinking Hooch and kissing messily. My friends weren't there. I stayed long enough to watch a frightening geezer with shaven head singing 'Delilah' – between verses he shouted, 'Come, on Chingford,' and 'I've got an enormous penis, by the way' – then left. What happened, I found out later, was that my friends turned up before me, found the place so young and loud it made them feel like voyeurs, and retreated to their usual pub, the Cricketers, in the Lanes, expecting me to follow them. But, being a bit diligent and stubborn, I stayed on the pier, and it's a good job that I did because that's how I saw Rose.

As I walked back along the pier the Fish & Chip Café button-holed me with vinegary breath, inveigled me in like a pierrot of old: Here, you, yes you. Listen up, you'll be interested in this, you look the type. This is where, more or less at least, Pinkie's mob in *Brighton Rock* have fish and chips, all except Spicer to be exact 'cos he feels sick, and Pinkie suggests ordering ice-cream for afters, and Dallow says, 'Stow it, Pinkie, we don't want ice-cream. We ain't a lot of tarts, Pinkie.'

'Roll out the Barrel' was playing on the tape as I went in, followed by 'Ma, He's Making Eyes at Me' as I clocked the laminated menu, 'The Hokey Cokey' as I ordered, 'On the Sunny Side of the Street' as I sipped my tea and 'Knees Up Mother Brown' as I lifted the pimpled vinegar bottle. But then – on the first, gently steaming forkful of white cod and batter, loaded with half a chip, shellacked with vinegar – the tape went mad, ripped off its lovable Cockney glad-rags, stuck on a ten-gallon hat and belted out 'Deep in the Heart of Texas'. The canon of East End balladry being finite, they had had to find something else to fill up the tape. Through this aural blather shimmered Rose, keeper of the cruets, a bit freckly and ginger, pigeon-toed, bony and virginal, in her green and white uniform with a name badge that said CHRISTELLE: 'Ketchup? Tartare sauce?'

I can no longer remember what the Rose of *Brighton Rock* looked like, in my mind's eye, before I saw the film of the book by the Boulting Brothers, John and Roy; I can't recall the image I'd constructed for her, pre-Carol Marsh. Carol Marsh, being such a perfect, dewy, blighted Rose, had wiped out any prior fancy when I first saw the film twenty-odd years ago. So when I saw Christelle I saw Carol Marsh, or rather Carol Marsh playing the character of Rose, Pinkie's devout dupe whom he must marry or kill, to stop her blabbing.

Carol is mousy and put-upon in the film, as the role demands, but when her face wasn't moving, when the still camera was on her, not the cine, she couldn't help looking what she was, even dressed for the part in her pinny and guileless make-up; she couldn't help looking beautiful. Whatever happened to Carol Marsh? Something bad, that was for sure. When I saw Christelle in her uniform, looking like Carol Marsh playing Rose, I saw *tristesse* in a drip-dry dress.

The week before my Saturday night on the Palace Pier I had sat in the flat of legendary film-maker Roy Boulting, and worked my way lingeringly through a box of velvety black and white prints of Carol Marsh. They had been taken during the shooting of *Brighton Rock* in 1947. In some she was with a very young Richard Attenborough,who played Pinkie Brown with such reined-in menace; in some she was on her own; in all she was both sad and beautiful. Roy said that hers was a sad story, a faint, tragic appendix to the phenomenon of *Brighton Rock*. But he wouldn't be drawn on precisely how or why her life had gone wrong. Her mishap and misery were not my property.

Roy and his twin brother John were two of the greats of British cinema. The furry cardboard box containing the still photographs of Carol Marsh lived on a shelf alongside dozens of other boxes casually marked with the names of classic films they made together from the thirties to the seventies. *Private's Progress, Carlton Browne of the F.O., I'm All Right, Jack, Brighton*

Rock . . . Charming, original, witty, perceptive films which in different ways bottled some of the essences of mid-century Englishness. Yet who had heard of Roy now?

I had been fortunate in knowing an old colleague and good friend of Roy's. Mary was my neighbour in south-west London. She had worked for some years as the Boulting brothers' secretary, and later for other famous names in British cinema, such as Frank Launder and Sidney Gilliat. I mentioned to Mary that it would be fascinating to talk to Roy about the making of *Brighton Rock*. She gave me his number and suggested that if I fixed up to see him she could come along too and we could make a day of it.

Roy was charming on the telephone. Yes, of course I could come up to see him. I should bring Mary and I should bring my girlfriend Miren ('She's a film buff and would be honoured to meet you, Mr Boulting,' I explained) and we would have a grand day. 'And one final thing,' he said. 'Don't call me Mr Boulting.'

The three of us drove to Oxfordshire on a humid May morning. The Chilterns steamed in a sub-tropical fret; cars wore sidelights at noon. Roy's flat, however, was cool and shady. Roy was tall and spare, with a full head of dark hair, wearing an orange roll-top shirt, slightly grubby chinos and battered loafers. He sat me in his black canvas director's chair, with ROY BOULTING written on the backrest in white letters. The room was hemmed in with shelves containing books and ring-binders and those boxes of stills from forty years' worth of movies.

Roy sat behind his desk, facing the room, and we talked initially of cricket. The Boultings were great cricket fans. Work at their offices in Berwick Street, and later Glebe Place, Chelsea, would practically come to a standstill during Test matches. One of them would turn on the television on the Thursday morning of a Test, and whoever wandered in would stick around until a roomful of people had gathered – and that would be it, more or less, till Tuesday afternoon. Mary said, 'If for any reason the broadcast was interrupted – to say war had been declared, for instance – Roy would turn to me and say, "Darling, ring up the BBC and ask them why on earth they have stopped the cricket."'

'Yes, dear,' said Roy. 'The idiocies of the Boulting brothers are memorialized in their films.' Miren, my girlfriend of the encyclopaedic film knowledge, racked her brains in vain for any cricketing scenes in their oeuvre. 'The *spirit* of cricket, dear,' said Roy, and suddenly we knew what he meant. He meant, in particular, one unplayable over of arcane drollery from *Carlton Browne of the F.O.*, in which two Whitehall mandarins – one of them played by Terry-Thomas – meet at the airport *en route* to the faraway colonial troublespot of Gallardia. We sat there for a few minutes trying to piece it back together. It seemed a special sort of effrontery to be correcting Roy when he had written the dialogue in the first place, but he didn't seem to mind.

We batted bits of this dialogue back and forth, then went to the village pub, where Roy had booked lunch in the restaurant. Our table was tucked inside the vast old fireplace and our Spanish waiter, Jesús, brought bottles of Macon Villages and plates of beef in ale and ham and eggs. Bright with wine, his hands moving like shadow puppets against the terracotta backdrop of the walls, Roy then rescripted, relit and reshot a defining moment, a moment of epiphany, from his childhood in Hove.

He and John had been born in Buckinghamshire, but when they were still very young the family moved to New Church Road, Hove, and a large house of stolid turn-of-the-century respectability. As was the norm, the everyday business of looking after the twins fell to a succession of nannies. Some were better than others. One in particular, formerly a dispatch rider in the Great War, was a sadist in stays. One morning the twins' parents left to take the train up to town, got as far as Hove

Station and realized they had forgotten something vital pertaining to their business in London. When they returned unexpectedly Roy was nowhere to be seen. 'Where is Master Roy?' demanded his mother. Master Roy was locked in an upstairs cupboard, where the nanny had intended leaving him for the best part of the day as punishment for cheeking her, or not polishing his shoes, or some such misdemeanour. The dispatch rider was dispatched forthwith.

But one nanny was never to be forgotten. She had a capacious bosom and a strange odour – camphor and scent, perhaps – which they grew to love. She believed religiously in the health-giving properties of sea air, regardless of the weather. And she harboured, in that spectacular bosom, a shameful secret: she loved Rudolph Valentino.

She was also a stickler for eating everything up: clean plates, clean minds. The twins enjoyed the challenge of hiding anything they didn't want to eat and getting rid of it later, and so battle was joined every mealtime. But this particular day there was no fun in it. They could both have stood up, carried their plates of boiled mutton, peas and cabbage to the sash window and thrown them down among the hoofs and hansoms of New Church Road, and Nanny would scarcely have noticed.

John looked at Roy and indicated his spoon. Roy looked at the spoon, which John tilted to reveal a tiny green boules-set of peas beneath. Roy nodded at the floor. John looked down to see a handful of cabbage on the carpet. Then they both looked at Nanny but, staring straight ahead, a smile playing around her lips, she appeared to be in some sort of euphoric waking coma. Then she spoke, slowly. 'Twins, suppose we don't go for a walk today.' They regarded her with wonder and pity. No meteorological extreme had ever been sufficient to persuade Nanny not to take them out for their walk. Hell would freeze over before she stopped taking them for their daily constitutional along the seafront as far as the peace statue and the border with Brighton (but *never* further, never into Brighton, which was known in the family as Sin City) and back again. 'Supposing', she went on, trying to sound casual, 'I took you to Brighton instead. To the pictures . . .'

Brighton? The pictures? The shock of hearing her utter these two words was profound. The twins looked at each other in amazement, then launched themselves at her, John at the right bosom, Roy at the left. 'Oh, Nanny!' they cried. Brighton was a Forbidden Place, fit only to be viewed from the safety of a passing carriage *en route* to the railway station. Movies were new and decadent, democratic and exotic, entirely beyond the pale for well brought up young gentlemen such as the Boulting boys.

But Nanny adored the pictures, as another might have an unadmitted weakness for port and lemon; and a picture had just opened at the splendiferous new picture palace, the Regent, next to the Clock Tower in Brighton, that starred a young actor who reduced her vitals to a state of delicious liquescence. She had to see it and she couldn't wait for her day off, even if it meant taking the children with her, into Brighton, risking her job and their moral well-being. 'Oh, Nanny!' The twins hugged themselves to her, breathed in great heady drafts of her singular smell through her starchy front. And then one of them – Roy or John, it doesn't matter – got canny, drew his head back, looked up into her shining eyes and asked: 'Does *Mummy* know about this?'

They took the bus from Hove into Brighton. To assuage her conscience Nanny made them travel on the open upper deck so they could take the fresh air for a few minutes at least. They got off at the Clock Tower and there, just down the hill in North Street, was the fabulous bowed frontage of the Regent picture palace, newly opened that year, 1921, with seating for 1,700 people, described by the *Brighton Herald* as 'the largest, finest, most artistic kinematograph establishment in the country, if not in the world'. Emblazoned across the front:

REX INGRAM PRESENTS WALLACE BEERY, ALICE TERRY AND RUDOLPH VALENTINO IN THE FOUR HORSEMEN OF THE APOCALYPSE. They were in awe, Roy, John and Nanny. Waiting to cross the road, the boys' hands in hers, they stared at the impossible, futuristic, illicit glamour of it all. *Rudolph Valentino!* said Nanny to herself. Roy remembered it cost 6d apiece for him and John. Inside the Wurlitzer organ boomed around the gloomy cavern, the carpet felt thick enough to reach their knees, the seats were like upholstered clouds. And then the organ sank, and the lights faded, and then the film itself . . .

Several months after meeting Roy I went to see *The Four Horsemen* for myself, to try to get a sense of what he and John must have felt. This was a ludicrous notion, of course, that I could hope to replicate their experience. But still. Just about the only way to see the film now is to book an editing suite at the British Film Institute and watch it on a Steenbeck editing machine, changing the reels yourself. As it turned out, the slot I booked fell on the day before the funeral of Princess Diana, when most of the country was sleepwalking its way through a collective nervous breakdown. The sun shone; the streets of London were chaotic but calm, as if in a dream. Valentino's funeral, too, in New York, had been touched with an awesome insanity. People had rioted on the streets of Manhattan, people had killed themselves with grief.

I settled in a windowless basement room with Miren and Mary. The film reels were stacked in eight silver circular canisters and we became our own projectionists. The black reels were big as a dinner plate and heavy as a marrow, and you had to press in on the rim as you transferred them to the machine lest the coiled strip of celluloid fall in an inverted cone and unravel. There was something intimate and collaborative about this process, as if we were bathing an infant for the first time and were terrified of dropping it. We had brought peppermints and apples and there was a festive air about us as we turned off the overhead light and cocked the switch to start the show.

I suppose I had regarded silent films as an essentially primitive form, an evolutionary step on the way to the finished article, the talkie. But the silent film, I realized now, was a wholly different, fragile and flickering phenomenon. The subtitles of *The Four Horsemen*, rendered in a typeface as elegantly curved as the façades of twenties picture houses, were no crude glosses on the action, but rills of poetic prose that occasionally burst in glorious torrents across the screen: 'In a world old in hatred and bloodshed, where nation is crowded against nation and creed against creed, centuries of wars have sown their bitter seed, and the fires of resentment smouldering beneath the crust of civilization but await the breaking of the Seven Seals of Prophecy to start a mighty conflagration . . .'

The film charts the redemptive passage of 'youthful libertine' Julio Desnoyers, played by a volcanic Valentino, from the fleshpots of Buenos Aires to the *ateliers* of Montmartre and, finally, the trenches of the western front where he dies a hero. The dance sequences, the Hogarthian interiors, were electric and sumptuous; the subtitles kept pinning you by the throat: 'The world was dancing. Paris had succumbed to the mad rhythm of the Argentine tango.' I carried the reels with increasing passion to the sprockets. The final reel, in which Desnoyers expires in a bomb crater, was no bigger than a side-plate.

Outside, at pavement level, the eyes of the people eating at outdoor cafés were a bit blanker than usual, as if Conquest, War, Pestilence and Death were stalking the sunny side of Charlotte Street that odd September week in 1997.

Outside, too, at Brighton's Clock Tower in 1921, Nanny stood with tears streaming down her face, tears of mourning for Desnoyers' death, of gratitude for Valentino's life. But the twins: the twins were radiant and privileged because they had seen their future and knew it.

*   *   *

104

Seventy-five years later, Roy's beef in ale was growing cold on his plate. The pub was empty, Jesús hovered. Outside, it had freshened and brightened, the thunder hadn't come as we had expected. Squadrons of young mothers wheeled pushchairs towards the gates of a primary school. Roy suggested we went back to the flat for afternoon drinks, and to hear the story of *Brighton Rock*.

The twins had just finished making a rather dull film called *Fame is the Spur*, in which Michael Redgrave rises from poverty to become prime minister, when out of the blue a chap rang from the film agents O'Brien, Linnit & Dunfee. A company part-owned by Terence Rattigan had acquired the film rights to Graham Greene's *Brighton Rock*. Rattigan had attempted a couple of film scripts but had been unhappy with the results. 'I don't think his heart's in it,' said the agent. 'It's probably more up your street.' The twins re-read a novel that on its publication eight years before had been a bestseller and *cause célèbre*, and made a happy discovery. Whatever else it might have been, *Brighton Rock* was film writing, something that could only have been done by someone interested in and knowledge-able about film. (I could bear this out myself as, the day before visiting Roy, I had sat watching the film with the book open on my lap, seeing how the fabric of film had been stitched from the template of text. It was remarkable how closely the film followed the book, borrowing dialogue, matching it more or less scene for scene till beyond half-way, when the film became more selective, telescoping, truncating and editing.)

The Boulting Brothers agreed immediately to buy the rights and to ask Greene himself to write the screenplay. Greene produced an excellent draft, based closely on the book but not afraid to depart from it for filmic imperatives. The co-credit on the finished film (and one of the 'facts' that people tend to remember about it), 'Screenplay by Graham Greene and Ter-ence Rattigan', is merely the result of contractual obligation.

The casting didn't run so smoothly, however. Looking

remarkably callow even for his twenty-four years, Attenborough in one important respect seemed the appropriate choice as Greene's Pinkie, the teenage mobster who gathers hell about him like a cloak as the book darkens. For Greene made Pinkie abjure alcohol and drink milk instead – like gangsters Greene had observed in a club near King's Cross Station – and no actor of the time looked more recently weaned than the absurdly youthful 'Dickie darling'. But after watching Attenborough play Pinkie in the stage play which preceded the film, Greene decided he wasn't right. 'Please do not use Richard Attenborough,' he wrote to the twins. 'He will never be able to convey the evil that's in Pinkie.'

After the film came out he was big enough to write them another letter: 'I am very grateful that you disregarded what I had to say about Richard Attenborough.' To Attenborough himself he posted off a copy of *Brighton Rock* with this inscription written on the flyleaf: *For my perfect Pinkie*. From the memorable opening shot of Pinkie's hands, playing obsessively with a length of string, knitting it into a cat's cradle with stiff, steepled fingers, Attenborough, with his soft-boiled-egg eyes, wove a tightening web of evil that remains one of British cinema's *tours de force*.

The book had been badly received in Brighton when it came out. Greene noted how the civic authorities had not taken kindly to the picture he painted of mobsters, extortion rackets and race gangs: 'It must have galled them to see my book unwittingly advertised at every sweetstall – "Buy Brighton Rock".' The film, which came out nine years later, could only add to the misrepresentation as far as Brightonians were concerned, hence the strange disclaimer which appears on screen at the beginning, over shots of the beach crowded with happy holidaymakers:

Brighton today is a large, jolly, friendly seaside town in Sussex, exactly one hour's journey from London.

But in the years between the two wars, behind the Regency terraces and crowded beaches, there was another Brighton of dark alleyways and festering slums. From here the poison of crime and violence and gang warfare began to spread until the challenge was taken up by the Police.

This is a story of that other Brighton – now happily no more.

In the spring of 1947, before filming started, Roy had spent three months in Brighton, staying with friends in Ovingdean while he worked on a shooting script. His research entailed much hanging around in pubs, dropping lavish hints about the old razor gangs and hoping someone would pick them up. There were plenty of turnip-nosed old soaks, of course, who claimed to have been in this or that mob, but Roy struck lucky when he was put on to a ferrety chap called Carl Ramón – 'See 'im in the corner? Wiv the wonky eye?' He was told he had carried the razor for the notorious Sabini gang. It's not easy, if you think about it, approaching a stranger in a pub and asking if he has ever been a violent criminal. Roy was one of the few people who could have pulled it off.

Once Ramón had established that Roy wasn't an undercover rozzer or a fantasist, Roy had him eating out of his hand, and for the next several weeks they ran the gauntlet of demob-happy servicemen as they diligently mapped what was left of the Brighton underworld, from the pre-twee Lanes to low-life haunts in the North Laine area and anonymous refuelling stops around the railway station. The drinks were usually on the house.

After the stiff-upper-lip output of the war years, the film was genuinely shocking to many people, the *Natural Born Killers* of its day. Proving that Roy and Carl had done their homework, the characters chewed gum and spat, wore wide-boy suits, spoke in working-class accents and used rhyming slang. Much of it was shot on the streets of Brighton during the long hot summer of 1947 – what's called 'stolen' filming, for which cameras are hidden and people going about their business on the streets have no idea that the chap running past is an actor. So real life went on in the background: downtrodden women pushing huge prams, cats stalking the hot pavements, lending a ghastly verisimilitude to the premeditated violence at the front of the screen, in the core of the fiction.

The film premièred at the Savoy Cinema in East Street, Brighton (where Greene had seen *his* first film, *Sophie of Kravonia*), late on the evening of 8 January 1948. A surprisingly modern-sounding PR exercise accompanied the screening, for the twins and the cast – all except Carol Marsh – came on stage afterwards and joshed with the audience.

The film was 'an unfortunate essay in brutality', according to the *Brighton & Hove Herald*, but the *Evening Argus* took a more progressive stance, dismissing the film's critics as élitist and reactionary: '*Brighton Rock*, the film which had its first showing last night and will soon be going round cinemas all over the world, has been described as bad publicity for the town. Those who raise these objections are the same people who prefer to attract the few and continually oppose plans which attract the crowds.' The national press was hysterical. The *Daily Mirror*'s film critic posted a health warning, requisitioning the centre spread to warn: 'This film must not be shown.'

The film saves its biggest departure from the book for the very end. The ending of the novel is as bleak as you will find in fiction. In a kiosk on the pier Pinkie, at Rose's request, has recorded on a vulcanite disc a message for her. She wants it as a keepsake of their wedding day, an expression of his love for her. But instead of whispering sweet nothings, what he has really said, in the sound-proof booth as she waits outside, is this: 'God damn you, you little bitch, why can't you go back home for ever and let me be?' In the film he says: 'What you *want* me to say is, I love you. Here's the truth. I hate you, you little slut. You make me sick. Why don't you get back to Nelson Place and leave me be . . .' Outside the booth, Carol Marsh looks radiantly adoring. For Rose, the record of Pinkie's voice, and his message of love, will be a tiny, warming flame amid the permafrost of a future without him. When she walks purposefully along the seafront towards Frank's place, the greasy rooming house where the gang lived, to retrieve the record, she is, according to the novel, walking towards the worst horror of all.

This is not an ending which translates into film, which is why Greene and the twins came up with another ending for their film. But while their celluloid ending was different from the book's, it was just as shocking. Unfortunately it no longer exists, and Roy could not remember what it was. He racked his brains, had more wine, lit another Dunhill. 'It shows', he said, never at a loss for words, 'just how much of one's life may be effaced from memory, the significant equally with the inconsequential.'

The reason their original ending was lost was that the film censor took exception to it. What could have happened, in this brief sequence, that was so unacceptable? Perhaps Carol Marsh performs hara-kiri on the Palace Pier with a sharpened prong of Brighton rock. The shot fades to bloodcurdling screams along the seafront, the credits are daubed in blood . . . Whatever it was, even Graham Greene failed to persuade the censor of the need for it to stay in and at very short notice a replacement scene had to be written and shot.

The result was hated with a vengeance by everyone concerned, not least by Greene himself. For him it was a cheap way out. For the twins it was a hasty, botched piece of film-making, against the clock, which in its mood and lighting looked as if it belonged in a different film altogether. Yet it is that very quality of strangeness which now lends it a haunting air. This is not the world as hitherto constituted in the film. Perhaps it is purgatory.

Carol/Rose is in a nunnery. The catarrhal priest who in the book solaces her by invoking the appalling strangeness of the mercy of God is replaced by a mother superior. A gramophone is handy in the room. 'He loved me,' says Carol, 'I'll show you he loved me. Mother, can I?' She gestures at the gramophone, puts on the disc, lifts the needle across and listens raptly. 'You asked me to make a record of my voice,' says Pinkie's voice. 'Here it is. What you *want* me to say is, I love you, I love you, I love you . . .' The record sticks, the film ends.

'Ketchup? Vinegar? Tartare sauce?' Christelle/Rose was bending towards me and I was back in my own version of purgatory, deep in the heart of Texas, the Fish & Chip Café, Palace Pier, Saturday night. Christelle's synthetic dress reached up to her neck, keeping the grease off her thin, talced body. 'Or brown sauce? Some people prefer it, even on fish.' Pinkie marked Rose down straight away as one of those girls who creep about as if afraid of their own footsteps. Christelle's pallor, her desire to please might easily get on your nerves. Or it might make you love her, depending on whether you've just suffocated someone to death with a stick of rock beneath the pier.

Christelle was fairer than Carol Marsh, but she looked the right age, about seventeen. Carol had been signed up by Rank for their charm school, which is why she appeared in *Brighton Rock* 'by permission of the J. Arthur Rank Organisation'. The school was supposedly a hothouse for new talent, though its efforts to create a production line of precocious starlets made but a single name – Diana Dors – of any note.

Amid the general opprobrium heaped on the film *Brighton Rock*, Carol attracted good reviews for her performance. It should have been the start of something, but it wasn't. The British Film Institute could find no record of Carol after 1966, when she appeared in a television programme called *Lord Raingo*: no press cuttings, no obituary. 'It's quite unusual, actually,' said the researcher, 'for someone to just disappear like that.'

'No brown sauce,' I said. 'Thanks – and are there some mushy peas?' I ordered mushy peas. 'Sorry, Thanks.' Flustered, Christelle departed, returned with a tub of lava-hot Swarfega. Failing hilariously to sound like shitkickers, a choir was now singing 'Home, Home on the Range'. I ate and left.

A woman hurried along towards the sea end of the pier, taking a last puff on a filterless cigarette and flicking the butt in an arc towards the waves. She wore a turban and a long maroon coat with moth-eaten fur collar, lugging a box the dimensions of a hatbox, but containing something heavier than a hat, from the evidence of her grimace and limp.

Roy, younger than I am now, bounced down the boardwalk, happy to be free of Carl Ramón after successive nights imbibing among the criminally inclined. A solid worker, old Carl, but Roy was enjoying the novelty of not having to mind his Ps and Qs lest a chisel be poked up his nostril.

Roy saw rain whipping in gusts across the pier, saw very few people about save the disappearing back of the bizarre-looking woman he had spied coming on to the pier. He was supposed to be researching that scene when Pinkie tries to get Rose to kill herself right on the end of the pier. She is saved between the stirrup and the ground, by the arrival of Ida, Dallow and the bogies. Pinkie leaps off the end of the pier and straight into hell. Roy turned his eyes into a camera lens, looked, squinted, paused to make a note or two in a tiny notebook, licking first the end of the miniature pencil, force of habit, just as he knocked his cigarettes on the tin before lighting them.

Suddenly he felt thirsty, put away notebook and pencil, turned up his collar against the gusting wind and rain, hurried on past the ghost train and the shooting gallery, and stepped into the bar near the end of the pier (occupying then approximately the same site as the karaoke bar now) for a quick one.

111

He ordered, turned round and observed that there were only two other souls in on this cold, grey weekday in early spring, both sozzled old-timers with polyhedral drinkers' noses. In such circumstances more than a single drink could turn into a depressing affair. He drained his glass briskly and left.

As he did so he looked up into the slanting rain and his eye was caught by a placard high up by a window next to the bar: MADAME BINNY, CLAIRVOYANTE. Though his hand was half in his pocket, on the point of withdrawing the notebook so he could continue the note-taking, he was happy to defer the moment. Madame Binny sounded suddenly so interesting as to be irresistible. In he went through the open door, into a small windowless room hung with swagged drapes and lined with ill-assorted chairs: half doctor's waiting room, he thought, half brothel. There was no one about. At the far end of the room was a small flight of steps leading to an opening hung on either side by velvet curtains. From beyond the curtains came the sound of paper rustling, then a sudden *cough, cough, cough!* Roy thought to himself: Smoker's cough.

He cleared his throat and called softly: 'Madame Binny?'

Beyond the curtains, all sound ceased. Then a head poked out, like a tortoise from its ramparts, wearing a turban. 'Who's that?'

Roy recognized the strange woman he had followed on to the pier. 'Are you Madame Binny?' he asked.

The head emerged further, followed by a moth-eaten fur collar, a body draped in a maroon overcoat and a bony hand holding a cigarette, from which a thread of blue smoke spiralled pleasingly. 'I am,' she said. 'Who wants to know?'

'Madame Binny, it is merely someone who has been persuaded that you have a talent for revealing . . . a talent, that is, for foretelling . . . am I right? And I wondered if you might spare the time to, er, practise your singular talents upon this curious passer-by.'

'I see.' She changed her tune now, sounded *faux*-posh: 'Will

112

you be so kind as to wait one minute, please?' She withdrew behind the curtains and Roy heard more rustling. Then: 'Please step this way.'

Roy climbed the steps, ducked through the curtains and into a small, windowless chamber lit by a single candle. As his eyes adjusted to the gloom he saw pictures of star signs on the walls around him; a table in front of him draped in pink velvet upon which flickered the candle; next to it a large clear glass globe on a plinth, shot with deep fissures of orange light from the flame. Madame Binny sat behind the table. She still wore the turban but the overcoat had been replaced with a burgundy velvet cape. She had appended large round gypsy earrings, smeared a postbox of vermilion lipstick around her mouth, and slipped heavy silver rings on her fingers, which now caressed the base of the crystal ball. 'Would you please sit down? I wasn't expecting anyone on a day like this, to be honest, dear. Now, what was it you was wanting?'

'I would like you to read my future, if you will.'

'Yes, dear, but—' and she indicated a tariff card he hadn't noticed on the wall. 'Half a crown for one hand, four shillings for two, ten shillings for both hands and a reading of the ball as well. The ball is *most* efficasey-ous.'

'I'll have ten shillings' worth,' said Roy and held out his hands.

The readings turned out to be vague in the extreme. 'Are you in love, my dear? Because if you are I can tell you it will all turn out for the best in the end. Trust me. Trust Madame Binny . . .' And so on.

Roy felt half embarrassed on Madame Binny's behalf, annoyed with himself for having thrown away ten shillings. He should have stayed in the bar next door, bought a round for the old soaks there – money better spent. Then Madame Binny peered wide-eyed at the crystal ball, suddenly rubbed its surface furiously. 'I thought I'd seen it wrong at first but there's no mistaking it,' she said. 'I don't know whether I should tell you this but I'm going to anyway. If you're on the beach in the next few weeks just keep your eyes open, will you? Just keep your eyes open.'

'Why?' said Roy, rather wearily.

'I'll say no more than that, but it may mean something important.'

Roy thought no more of this, assuming it to be part of the rehearsed patter, and more or less forgot about Madame Binny. Three weeks or so later they had started filming and the weather could not have been better, not a single day's shooting lost to rain – blue skies, high temperatures, warm enough to swim in the sea even in June in that glorious summer of 1947. They rented rooms in the Grand Hotel to use as the production office, and on this particular morning it was so hot that an air of Latin laziness had settled upon everybody, cast and crew alike. 'How would you like wearing this bloody suit all day long?' said a sweating William Hartnell.

Roy paced restlessly, trying to jolly the troops, with little success. He decided it was that sort of day – they came along sometimes and it was best to go with the flow. He would go for a swim. After his swim he fashioned a pillow from his shirt and lay there watching people enjoying themselves around him. A man walked right past Roy on his way down to the water and Roy absent-mindedly watched him go. The man waded into the sea and forced his way through the people at the water's edge. Roy lost sight of him for a second or so, then picked him up again beyond the cordon of bodies as he launched himself into a competent-looking front crawl.

The man cruised about for a minute or so, then disappeared under the water. Roy waited for him to come up a few feet in front of where he had been, but there was no sign of him. Roy rocked forward on to his knees for a better look. Perhaps he had changed direction underwater. But no one was there. Roy suddenly felt sick. He stood up. The swimmer had definitely not surfaced. He sprinted down to the water, jumping over

114

bodies, and plunged underwater at the spot where he calculated the man disappeared.

He fumbled about, feeling rather than looking in the frothy sea, came up for air, had another go. And this time he found the man, felt the bulk of his shoulders, was slapped by his hand. He tried to drag him up above the surface but was not strong enough so he waved and shouted for help. Some people heard him over the general din and suddenly everyone in the vicinity had intuited a crisis, and the man was taken from Roy's arms and conveyed on a wave of goodwill to the beach.

The man did not come round, despite the increasingly frantic attentions of a doctor and ambulance crew. Roy sneaked a look through the thicket of legs. The man's lips were blue, snot of an alarming green colour was trailing from his mouth. Wiping away the snot, the doctor had another go. Roy felt sick. But then – and it must have been fifteen minutes at least, if not twenty, since they took him from the water – the man spluttered and stirred and people cheered.

Twenty years later Roy was down in Brighton, strolling on the pier, when he saw a sign on a kiosk: UNLOCK THE SECRETS OF YOUR SIGNATURE WITH WORLD-FAMOUS GRAPHOLOGIST MISS BINNY. AS SEEN ON TV.' The young woman was reading a magazine and posting ice-cream into her mouth. 'Copy a few lines of this out, then,' she said, barely looking up, and she handed him a mushy verse. Roy could have made a better reading of his signature himself, but he didn't mind. 'Miss Binny, thank you,' he said. 'And may I ask, are you related to Madame Binny?'

She started back, looking suspicious and amazed, as if he were possessed of the gift of clairvoyance himself. 'Why do you ask? How do you know?'

'I had', said Roy, 'a great admiration for your mother.'

I hadn't expected to find Carol Marsh. The general feeling was that she had drifted away somewhere a long time ago. But then a reporter on the *Argus* gave me her phone number.

115

Carol lived in Bloomsbury but we arranged to meet, at her suggestion, on the lower concourse of Canary Wharf station. The last time I had seen her she wore a spotted dress and tears glistened on her cheeks as she listened to Pinkie's voice saying 'I love you . . .' She said on the phone, 'You'll recognize me from the blue woollen coat.' In fact I recognized the sad, crinkly-eyed smile, intact after fifty years. Rose worked as a waitress in Snow's café. Carol and I drank tea in the Canary Wharf Café Rouge.

She had made a few films after *Brighton Rock*. 'People kept telling me, "When the next film comes out you'll be a star forever." But it never happened.' She had done lots of theatre and radio and now she lived a reclusive life, 'with no one to please and no one to hurt me.'

She was seventeen when she made the film, but by her own reckoning had an emotional age of about ten. Like Rose, she had been dreadfully preyed upon and *Brighton Rock* was an unhappy memory. 'People were very, very cruel. Why didn't they just leave me alone?' I said I thought she was luminous in the film and she replied that the thought of how good she might have been crucified her now.

'I've never seen the film and I couldn't bear to. I could not. All I've seen are when I've been sitting at home and clips come on the TV. I was riveted by one shot of me running down the pier and saying, "Pinkie!" I thought, My God what a sweet little girl. So naturally sweet.'

I asked Carol to sign my copy of the novel. I had in mind a variation on Greene's inscription to Attenborough: 'From your perfect Rose', but Carol said this would be big-headed.

She wrote: 'It was lovely meeting you. From "Rose".'

Chapter Seven

The Meeting Place was visible from the windows of my room. In the mornings I would usually be woken by the scraping of poles and flapping of tarpaulins as they put up the windbreaks. Sometimes I would be up early enough to see the café before the windbreaks had gone round, looking vulnerable and incongruous, like a poop deck without its ship. This early, before the sun was more than an unseen influence, sea and sky were the faintest mauve and hard to distinguish. Then you wished that Brighton might remain poised just there, in those proportions of colour and light and temperature, but then the world turned and fell headlong into the day, as it always did, leaving sadness in the air, as it invariably did.

If you mounted a camera in my window and recorded a day at the Meeting Place it might be like the cycle of a flower. At dawn it was small and tight but then it responded as if to the light, flexing and spreading, the shutters opening and the windbreaks going up. And the insects started hovering, brightly coloured, in ones and twos, in running singlets, on in-line skates, in pushchairs. The Lord of Brighton, lisping pugilist Chris Eubank, might even jog past, his skin black as paint against his brilliant white running gear, his knees encased in cushioned supports. The insects turned into a storm as the day aged; and then they died, and the café folded into itself, the tarpaulins disappearing into a shed, the shutters going up, the moon rising, scattering fragments of brilliant light on the sea.

I witnessed this cycle from my windows, often through binoculars, standing well back from the sill so the light didn't reflect from the lenses. What I learned was that the daily cycle was not quite over with the rising of the moon: as the moon slid across the sky and the light slid across the sea, moths gathered round the sleeping café and fluttered sadly there.

At night the environs of the café, and the statue next to it, was a trolling ground, where gay men went for urgent, anonymous, near-wordless sex with strangers. The statue was delicate and sexy, erected just before the First World War and showing the winged figure of Peace balancing upon a globe, her gown slipped down to expose her breasts, holding aloft an olive branch.

No one referred to the peace statue by the name of its dedicatee, Edward VII. Edward VII! The man gave his name to respectable townhouses, stiff collars and a stuffy, sepia-tinted notion of the past. Yet here was a supple, sexy thing, supposed to sum up a chinless skirt-chaser who hid behind a beard. Weird! Brightonians cared for her. Once, the council had erected scaffolding to clean her and left it up overnight. Someone had climbed it and stolen the olive branch, snapped it off. A big hoo-ha followed and a sculptor was commissioned to make good the damage. Occasionally someone threw an inner tube or tyre over her arms or wings, so she looked sad as a dog with a tin can tied to its tail. But, within a day or two, someone had always climbed her and removed the affronting object.

This bronze figure is the finest piece of municipal statuary I know of in England. The usual, turgid kind is summed up by the figure of Queen Victoria, along the seafront in Hove. Wearing a crown and holding a sceptre, old bootface is looking out to sea, deliberately shunning the town whose spirit offended every fibre of her being. She did the same in Reading – admittedly with more reason – stipulating that her statue should

118

face towards London, away from the town centre, because she didn't care for the place. Well, lots of people didn't care for her and her tenacious legacies. It was time for someone accidentally on purpose to begin knocking her off her perches.

In the shadow of these statues, men collided in the night. They swam unsteadily in the half-light from the moon and the fairy bulbs strung from the lampposts; they looked grainy, as if comprised of television dots. Some loitered and some circled until they reached their points of intersection. You knew – assumed – they spoke; you cursed the binoculars for not having the power of amplification as well as magnification.

What did they say? One nodded, they moved off together. They went on the beach behind the café, where I had washed egg yolk off my hands before handling the portrait of Guil Shakspeare. The beach shelved steeply here. Their legs disappeared, then one of them shot sideways, slipping on the pebbles – I heard the crunch, all the way up here in this attic room in the dark – and the other steadied him with his arm, touched him kindly, this person he did not know. They disappeared and did not reappear, not, at least, at the point where they had gone down; like ducks bobbing up yards from where they dived, they made you fear they had drowned. And so I watched them, but only so far. They fell out of sight, into a closed world where I could not follow.

You couldn't write about Brighton and not mention gays. Down here, by traditions of tolerance and force of numbers, homosexuals were assimilated, accepted, a more significant minority than anywhere else in Britain, if not in Europe. Many of Brighton's best pubs and clubs were predominantly gay. Single women in Brighton said that at dinner parties they were invariably disappointed in their hope of meeting eligible heterosexual men. The pink pound was strong, provision for AIDS sufferers was second to none. Gays weren't some miserable, hidden sub-section of society, but spanned the social spectrum. There were sunbed and medallion gays, separatist gays, wealthy gays, actorly gays and writerly gays, leather gays, San Francisco moustache-and-checked-shirt gays, men you wouldn't dream were gay, sad, furtive gays and body-pierced gays.

Of the men who habitually drank in the Grosvenor, more than half were gay. But then you wouldn't necessarily know which was which just by looking and listening, as two of the campest drinkers were in fact straight (one of them was a transvestite). Sometimes they spoke in polari, the gay slang of the fifties and sixties so daringly used by Kenneth Williams and Hugh Paddick on the radio show *Round the Horne*. 'Bona' meant good, 'lallies' were legs, a 'palone' was a woman, 'vada' was to look, 'trolling' was cruising for sexual partners, 'riah' was hair (spelled backwards). Back in fifties Brighton, when somebody was wearing a noticeably bad wig they used to say, 'Riah by Fludes,' Fludes being a local carpet shop.

Using polari was a joke now, but it had evolved as a necessarily secret form of communication. In those days exposure as a homosexual probably meant losing job, home and friends, and often resulted in a prison sentence. Being gay was as bad as being a delinquent or an immigrant, a Communist or a prostitute. Bosses, landladies, doctors, neighbours could seem like spies bent on the unmasking and punishment of deviants. The slightest detail might give the game away, so you could never relax. Were those cufflinks a bit much? Did I show I was bored when that woman was talking to me? Did I mince or lisp when I got drunk last night?

But in Brighton you didn't need to tiptoe terrified around the edges of your own life, for Brighton was a sanctuary for England's miserable and terrified gay community. Perhaps it was true that it had never lost that relish for high campery which the Regency fops brought to town, but its acceptance of gays was principally a function of its wider tolerance of human diversity. In Brighton women worked as petrol attendants and boys danced cheek-to-cheek, and nobody gave a shit.

I misread this gay thing. I assumed that, in Brighton at least, heterosexuals and homosexuals now inhabited the same world. As gays had found their freedom, and now stood in the beautiful Brighton sunshine, I assumed they would be willing to talk about the dark days when they had skulked in the shadows, fearful of being denounced. But then I discovered that their freedom could only ever be partial in a world that would always be alien in such a fundamental respect. The only place where they were really happy, really themselves, was in a parallel world all but invisible to heterosexuals.

This parallel reality had some of the qualities of the psychics' spirit world. It was there, all around you, but you had to have the requisite sensory equipment to pick it up. Just occasionally it might be made manifest, as on the occasions I had seen drag shows in the Oriental. Here I had been amazed by a sense of separateness, of people collectively relaxing, looking, talking, feeling in subtly different ways from the external world which even in Brighton remains predominantly heterosexual. Gays might love creating a pastiche of their world, might camp it up in the pub and have a good vada of your lallies, but when you said, 'Please may I be admitted to your world as an honorary member, just for a quick look round?' the shutters generally came down.

The trolley trolling story was a good example of this. Somebody in the Grosvenor had told me that Waitrose in the Western Road was a major trolling ground, for both gays and straights, and that a mute language of desire had developed whose vocabulary was what you put in your shopping trolley. A man introduced to me in the pub as Josie Bosnia assured me that this was the case, that he himself had occasionally participated and understood enough of the shopping-trolley language to be able to translate it. He would gladly take me up there one Saturday between about four and five in the afternoon, when most of this trolley trolling went on.

The notion of this language was intriguing, not to say

hilarious. Was it crudely pictive, like early cave paintings? Did an aubergine and two onions in your basket mean you were an active gay looking for a partner to penetrate? Did a doughnut mean you wanted to be penetrated? Or was it more allusive, a video and a TV dinner for one indicating simply that you were single, lonely and looking for someone to watch a film with? Josie Bosnia wouldn't say. I would have to wait and see. Josie owned a small hotel and said to pop round sometime and we would fix up a firm date to go to Waitrose.

A week or so later I happened to be passing Josie's hotel and decided to call in. The door to the lobby was locked so I rang the intercom buzzer and had an awkward metallic conversation with an extremely wary Mr Bosnia, who seemed to have forgotten our meeting in the pub. Finally he appeared inside, shuffling towards the glass door, peering suspiciously. He had no recollection of any conversation about trolley trolling in Waitrose. It was extremely unlikely in any case that he would know about such things because he was virtually celibate these days. He conceded that he went in the Grosvenor occasionally and that a version of the alleged conversation conceivably took place when he was extremely drunk, but if so he almost certainly concocted a tale that was wildly exaggerated where it wasn't made up. In any event, he was not at all interested in helping me. (This, by the way, was but the beginning of a fruitless search for the truth about trolling and trolley language in Waitrose. Perhaps not wishing to sound out of touch, many people said they had heard of it, but no one had actually done it, knew how it worked.)

At the time I thought little of Josie Bosnia's rejection. When people are doing you favours it is their prerogative to change their minds. But gradually I began to see a pattern in the way I was being treated by gays whose lives I wished to peer into. I was told I really should speak to an old queen known as Lady Precious Stream, who was described to me as Brighton's very own Quentin Crisp – well into his eighties, still outrageously flamboyant, with fifty years behind him as a drag artist in London's East End and on the south coast. The stories, my dear! A friend called Graham said he would be an intermediary, set up a meeting, preferably in Lady Precious's flat, which was a miasma of scent and feather boas. First, though, could I write a letter explaining my intentions. So I did this, being careful to include a promise not to reveal her true identity in anything I wrote, and Graham passed the letter on. After a few days I heard back: she was not interested in talking. Lady Precious Stream had dried up.

This pattern repeated itself with several other people who agreed to talk and then backed off. Ever obliging, my friend Graham said he would try to come up with some more names. And then it dawned on me. I didn't need anybody else. 'It's you,' I said. 'We've been trying to find interesting people and all the time it's been staring us in the face. I'll talk to *you*.' We were in the Grosvenor at the time. Graham rolled his eyes and looked at his lager and I thought even *he* was going to turn me down for a second. Then he said, 'All right. But I have to have a drink in front of me. And I can't be doing with tape recorders or notebooks.'

After he had talked to me, over several evenings and pints of lager, he said: 'There. I've told you things I've never told anyone else.'

One evening around this time I was sitting at the bar of the Grosvenor with Roger and I happened to mention the Trunk Murders of 1934, far and away Brighton's most notorious murder case. The barmaid that night was an elderly lady called Irene who for fifty years had been a landlady in various pubs and clubs in Brighton and still kept her hand in by working odd shifts here and there. The stories she could tell, my dear! Anyway, she overheard me mention the Trunk Murders and said she remembered them vividly, not least because her family had lived in Kemp Street, next to the murderer. 'But that's nothing,' she said. 'Everybody knows about Toni Mancini and the bodies in the trunk. But have you heard about the murder at the Blue Gardenia? I was working there the night it happened . . .'

Irene promised to tell me the whole, voluptuous, sordid, febrile tale of the Blue Gardenia. I just had to give her a call and arrange a convenient time. I was excited by this. Murder was emblematic of something Brightonian. It was stamped through Greene's *Brighton Rock*. The *kind* of killing the town attracted set it apart from other English towns. In his famous essay, 'Decline of the English Murder', first published in 1946, George Orwell lamented the passing of the quintessential English murder, a poisoning perpetrated with cunning by an intensely respectable dentist or solicitor living in a semi in the suburbs. But Brighton had never gone in for that kind of killing.

The Trunk Murders were a Brightonian masterpiece of macabre improbability. They were the product not of Orwell's late lamented 'stable society where the all-prevailing hypocrisy did at least ensure that crimes as serious as murder should have strong emotions behind them', but of anonymity, seediness and transience, the invisible scurf on England's stiff collar. On Derby Day, 6 June 1934, a brown canvas trunk was deposited at the left-luggage office in Brighton railway station. When it started to smell unpleasantly, a policeman was summoned to open it. Inside he found a woman's body with the head, arms and legs sawn off. The torso was wrapped in brown parcel paper and tied with sash cord. Written on the edge of the paper in blue pencil was the end of a word: 'ford'.

Next day the legs were discovered folded into a suitcase at King's Cross Station. The head and arms were never found, though the word in Brighton – still – is that they were thrown into the sea from the end of the Palace Pier. A man reported seeing a severed head in the surf at Black Rock, which he said was carried back out to sea on the tide. This case, known as the First Brighton Trunk Murder, has never been solved. The identity of the victim and the murderer, the cause of death and the motive, remain unknown.

Also in June 1934, in a basement at 47 Kemp Street, a row of small, dilapidated terraced houses mostly converted into flats, less than half a mile from the railway station, there lived a waiter called Toni Mancini, also known – according to which accounts of the case you read – as Luigi Mancini, Toni England, Toni English, Cecil Lois England, Jack Notyre and Antoni Pirillie. Despite his swarthy looks, his job and his portfolio of Italianate names, Mancini had no Italian antecedents and had never been further south than the end of Palace Pier.

He had an unusual flatmate in Kemp Street: the dead body of a forty-two-year-old dancer and prostitute called Violette Kaye, aka Violet Saunders and Joan Watson, which, perhaps by eerie coincidence, he was keeping in a trunk. Violette had died several weeks earlier in another basement flat, at 44 Park Crescent off the Lewes Road. Mancini had put her in a trunk, stuck the trunk on a trolley and with the help of two unwitting accomplices (did either of them say to Mancini: 'Christ, this is heavy. What you got in here then – a body?') wheeled her to Kemp Street.

Mancini first heard of the torso at the railway station from a fellow-waiter at the Skylark Café on the Lower Promenade, near West Street, where he worked. He felt sick with fear, and worked out the rest of the day convinced Violette had somehow been stolen and dismembered. Imagine, then, his joy, upon returning to Kemp Street to find Violette intact, undisturbed!

The body of Violette Kaye was eventually discovered after Mancini had fled to London and his flat in Kemp Street was searched. He was arrested in Lewisham and his trial for murder started at Lewes in December 1934. His defence, conducted by Norman Birkett KC, was a novel one. Mancini had found Kaye battered to death in the flat they shared in Park Crescent. She was a known prostitute and Mancini assumed she had been killed by a client. He didn't, however go to the police because he was afraid that with his criminal record – he had several convictions for petty theft – he would not be believed. Accepting this explanation, the jury returned a not guilty verdict. On 28 November 1976, in the *News of the World*, Mancini, then aged sixty-eight, admitted: 'Before I die I want to set the record straight. The verdict was wrong. I did kill Violette Kaye.'

Everyone knew about the Trunk Murders, but who had heard of the Blue Gardenia slaying? A few people said they had, but in that vague, don't-quote-me kind of way. Or perhaps they just thought they had heard of it. Simply the name 'Blue Gardenia' conjured a heyday of heroic seediness, made it sound like a familiar case. All I knew was that it had been a gay bar, surely somewhere off the beat, in a basement thick with smoke and illicit yearning. In the Blue Gardenia the worlds of gays and of murder, the unspoken and the unspeakable, had intersected momentarily and catastrophically.

I was impatient to talk to Irene properly about it. We arranged a meeting, which Irene cancelled at the last minute. We made another date – cancelled again. And I realized that she had changed her mind about talking to me; that, again, I was being cold-shouldered. Perhaps the Blue Gardenia had never existed, or only in that parallel universe to which I was unable to gain admittance. A veil had twitched, but now it had fallen back into place.

About the time the Blue Gardenia murder would have happened, had it happened – that is, in the late fifties or early sixties – in the small market town of Hassocks, some ten miles north of Brighton, a young boy was spending his last few pennies on a cup of tea at the end of a long hot summer's afternoon. He had caught the train from Brighton that morning with the intention of going all the way to London, but when the train

126

stopped at Hassocks he had lost his nerve and got off. He had mooched around for half a day looking for half a chance, but it was a dead sort of place, at least from the waist down. By spending the last of his money on a cup of tea he was burning his boats; if he still wanted to get up to London, or even back to Brighton, he would have to hide in the toilet and run for it at the other end. But he didn't care.

He went into the café near the station, debated between having lemonade and tea, chose tea, and sat down at a table next to the window, with a view of the rest of the café. He drank the tea slowly, so it grew discernibly colder between sips, and looked at the men there. Those who weren't old enough to be his father were certainly old enough to be his grandfather. They were rheumy-eyed and grey-whiskered, they had hacking coughs and smoked incessantly. The boy thought of the way the flesh on an old man went grey, so it looked dead. He had seen plenty of old, ill-nourished, half-poisoned flesh. But his father's flesh was brown and tough. He pictured the way the small knife had slid across the flesh of his father's forearm when he tried to stab him. There had been blood, but not much, which he regretted. Still, they must be looking for him. But no one was looking at him in this café, and he was glad because they were disgusting. What he was required to do was not disgusting at all, he could enjoy it, but whom he was required to do it with was frequently insupportable. So he was relieved not to be noticed, even if it meant he would have no money tonight.

But then a man walked into the smoky café and the boy knew pretty soon his luck had changed. The man was close in age to the men around him, but there the similarity ended. Despite the heat, he wore a belted woollen overcoat. There were drops of sweat on his upper lip and on his forehead. He was very tanned, looked foreign, Italian maybe. He was fat, but it was a sleek, prosperous fatness. He took a seat and stayed there, expecting to be served. The men around him coughed and smoked, didn't acknowledge him at all. It was as if they didn't see him, and perhaps they didn't. Perhaps they saw nothing at all any more. Minutes passed.

The owner was in the kitchen at the back, listening to the racing results on the radio. The boy looked at his tea, swilled it around the cup – stone cold now, still half an inch to go. The man loosened the belt of his coat, eased the coat open, rattled a shoe on the lino and shifted his chair. He was going to leave, but then he saw the boy. He stared at the boy quite openly, intently, as if sure that the other men in the café didn't count, would be powerless to intervene. The boy liked being looked at in this way, felt the power of the man. He wondered what it would lead to. He was ready for whatever that may be. The man nodded at the boy, stood up and left the café without being served. The boy followed, as the man had known he would.

Perhaps the man just wanted a quick toss-off in the bushes for a couple of quid, but the boy didn't think so. The man had time and money, perhaps a lot of money. The man was worth being obliging to. The man crossed the station forecourt to the left-luggage office. He came out with two suitcases, approached the boy and spoke to him for the first time. 'Is this too heavy?' He handed the boy the smaller of the cases. The boy tried it, said no. 'Good,' said the man. 'Follow me.' He waddled as he carried the heavier case. Two paces behind, the boy watched him struggling along the pavement. Sweat flicked off his forehead and on to the still-warm pavement. With a half-glance behind him to the boy, the man turned into the entrance of the coaching inn, rang a bell at the reception desk just inside. As he waited for someone to come he turned to the boy and said, 'You're my son, by the way.' The boy thought, *I know that.*

The room had two single beds. The man said, 'I'll give you ten pounds.' This was a lot of money, and the boy smiled. 'But I expect my money's worth.' The man instructed the boy to undress while he watched. Then the man undressed. The boy was energetic and gave the man his money's worth. It was getting dark outside. They could hear laughter and the clinking of glasses coming from the bar downstairs. The boy reached for his clothes and began to dress. Now he had £10, things became possible. Up to London or back to Brighton? He still didn't know. He supposed that if he went back to Brighton he would have to face the music, sooner or later. You couldn't go around stabbing your own father and expect to get away with it. But London was difficult. He didn't know the place, had never been there, would scarcely know where to start, except for the obvious.

The man lay in bed watching the boy dressing, as he had watched him undress. The boy buttoned up his flies and tied his jumper round his waist by the arms and asked for his money, holding his hand out. 'Later,' said the man. 'I'm tired. What's the hurry?' The boy said his mother would be missing him. She knew he had gone to Hassocks. People might be looking for him. He thought of threatening to scream, but as he looked at the man, lying there in bed, he saw his eyelids drooping, and decided on another plan. 'Just calm down,' breathed the man sleepily. 'I'll make it worth your while.'

Within five minutes the man was snoring. The boy stood over him, waved a hand right in front of the man's face. He went over to his overcoat, draped over a chair, took out his wallet and took all the money there was in it. He let himself out of the room and forced himself to walk quietly out of the hotel. He passed the receptionist, who smiled at him. The boy ran to the station. There was a train to London in seven minutes. He bought a ticket and waited anxiously for the train to arrive. Once on board he went straight to the toilet and counted his takings: £120 in tenners, fivers and one-pound notes. It was an unimaginable fortune.

The boy was fourteen and had been having sex with men

for money since he was nine and a man had approached him in a public toilet on the seafront. It was just tossing men off with his hand for a long time, or having it done to him, and he enjoyed it mostly. Then a man tried something different. The man asked him to hide his genitals between his legs, so he looked like a girl, then simulated vaginal penetration of the boy, thrusting away between his legs, hurting him, banging on the walls of the cubicle with his fists. When the pain and noise were reaching a crescendo the door of the cubicle was kicked in and both of them were arrested by the police, who had been staking out the toilets.

This was the first the boy's parents knew of what he got up to. The boy's father, who was a merchant seaman and away from home for long stretches, thrashed him with a belt. It was a blood-curdling event. The father actually locked the door of the boy's bedroom before setting about him. Downstairs, the mother busied herself in the kitchen with the radio turned up. Afterwards, the boy spent twenty-four hours locked in his bedroom without food. At the suggestion and recommendation of the police, the boy's father sent him to a psychiatrist in New Church Road, Hove, who specialized in deviancy.

The psychiatrist asked the boy to describe exactly what he had been required to do by the men he had gone with. As he listened to the boy's prosaic catalogue of mechanical acts, the psychiatrist seemed to get excited. In a thick voice he ordered the boy to take off his trousers and, unable to stop himself, he pushed the boy face first against the wall and buggered him. 'Like *this*, like *this*?' he screamed as he did it. The boy escaped and ran home. His mother was out – probably on her way to collect him from the psychiatrist in New Church Road.

In his bedroom the boy picked up a penknife and waited for his father to return from his lunchtime session at the pub. He didn't intend to kill him, just to hurt him. In the event he hardly did that. His father was drunk, but managed to deflect the blow with his forearm. The boy had then run to the station and caught the London train, getting off at Hassocks. In London he went to the only place he knew of, the Dilly, and made money the only way he knew how. He was pretty by then, incredibly so. He spent some of his new-found fortune on clothes, looked like Alain Delon. He didn't need to take on the rancid, the halitotic, the furtive, the ones with alopecia, the ones with wives, with sons the same age as him, the ones who lived with their mothers, the ones who cried and wished to kiss him on the lips. He liked the sort he had made happy in the coaching inn in Hassocks, who carried around wads of money, wore belted overcoats. He liked cars, doing it in cars, on leather, the smell of leather and of mahogany. He had done it in the back of a chauffeur-driven car with the chauffeur there in the front, affecting not to notice, not to see, not to smell, not to hear. He was passed on, like a new brand of cigar. He stayed in hotels with people who were famous. He was the regular companion of a peer of the realm and of a psychopathic gangster.

He would be summoned by the gangster, along with three or four others. They would wait in a car outside a Soho club, sometimes for hours. Sometimes they were told they could go; a henchman would open the car door and say, 'Go on, fucking scarper,' without seeing the gangster at all. Usually, though, they got the word at some stage in the evening. Then they would be taken down into the club, into the cigar smoke and menace, eyes stinging with the smoke, and be sat at a table near the gangster. The gangster would joke, 'Vimto all round,' and his friends would laugh. The gangster might make clucking noises, and they would have to cluck back. 'Come on, chickens,' he would say, 'come on, you fucking *poultry*, sing for your supper,' and the friends would laugh.

But he meant it, the boys would have to cluck like chickens, there and then, with stinging eyes and trembling hearts, amid the cigar smoke and menace, and it seemed as if the whole world were laughing at them then. Or the gangster was serious, wouldn't look at them the whole evening, until he pointed his cigar at the chosen one. Sometimes the gangster chose more than one at a time, which was better, safety in numbers. Going to bed with the gangster was like being locked in the lion enclosure for the night. He liked scratching their backs until he drew blood. He grew his fingernails for the purpose and licked off the blood afterwards, liking the commingled taste of sweat and meat.

In the morning the boys stole the silver teaspoons from the breakfast tray brought in by the liveried bellboy. Sometimes the bellboy was about the same age as the boys and the gangster would make suggestions, raise his eyebrows and say, 'Eh, boys?' to the boys. The bellboy would stammer, 'Enjoy your breakfast sir,' and back out of the room. The gangster might say, 'What if I want *you* for breakfast?' and cackle smokily as the door closed. The gangster enjoyed throwing back the sheets so young bellboys would see the streaks of blood there, see what they were missing. If, however, the bellboy was old, grey and stooped with red-rimmed eyes, the gangster would fold a ten-bob note into his top pocket and say, 'There you go, cock. Have one on me.'

The boy reckoned he enjoyed protection from the gangster. How else was it that he slipped like a sprat through the net the police spread every so often over Piccadilly Circus? Uniformed officers looked through him on Broadwick Street. In the toilets the plain-clothes men standing urineless for long periods mysteriously overlooked his allure in favour of shabby starers and flashers. Then one day it changed. Perhaps he had grown too old, too knowing in the face, too padded on the hips. Perhaps his technique, thrilling and thoughtful as it was, had grown stale. Now he would wait in the car and not be summoned. Or if he was, if he made it as far as the club, he would get no further but be dispatched upward into the night, back to the West End trolling grounds of the Dilly and Soho.

The law's *agents provocateurs* began to stare at him rather than through him. He took more care, looked left and right and up and down, but you can never take enough care when they've marked your card. It happened, as he knew it would, with a punter who'd been hardly worth it in the first place – a fat Russian diplomat with body odour and sepia-tinted fingers. No money to speak of, bad teeth, bad smells. The copper was in the next cubicle, who knows?, having a crafty J. Arthur himself while he waited. The Ruskie's mouth opened and closed soundlessly when the door was kicked in. The Ruskie shoved himself away and buttoned himself up and the boy shrugged.

The policeman had a soft round face that the boy could have stroked, strangely enough. In a moment of madness this was what he almost did. But then the Russian fled and the policeman had the boy's arm up behind his back so it was almost breaking and even then he could feel the copper's breath, if he turned his head could have kissed his cheek, and who knew what then might have happened, fireworks or dungeons, exalted life or a kind of death. 'Nice out, in't it?' said the boy instead, gasping through the pain, and then, changing voice: 'Yes, well, put it away, there's a policeman coming.'

At West End Central they charged him with procuring and discovered they had netted a runaway, a juvenile wanted for a serious assault on his own father. 'You don't have to tell him, though?' asked the boy helplessly. 'Please don't tell me Dad.' Then they knew they had him, could hurt him, pin him to pain like a fly to a board, dismantle him, this snake-hipped kid with his arch eyes and mocking mouth. They called Brighton Police, who went round to see the father, then they slung the boy in a cell with a drunk where he huddled and shivered all night. And in the morning the hatch over the small barred window in the cell door slid open and the boy saw, divided into strips by the bars, the face of a man with a score to settle.

He was beaten now. All the knowingness he had acquired, the manipulativeness, the humour and the art of provocation, the smile and the wink, the laugh and the shrug, his ways of winning against the world, all went when he saw that face. The face took him away, back to orderliness, propriety and wholesomeness, short back and sides and chops for tea, back to thrashings with a belt for filthy little queers. Back to Brighton, and what a very odd sort of Brighton it was, a dungeon in the basement of England. This time the locked bedroom door was a necessity as well as a punishment, buying time for the bruises and cuts to fade from their initial, unmissable luridness. The father administered a double dose, for the knifing as well as the poncing. The mother listened to the radio, *Round the Horne* turned up so the voices distorted. But the father hadn't finished with the boy, in fact had barely started.

The father had talked to a priest as well as to the police. Between them they mapped a course for the boy. He would plead guilty, in juvenile court, to the charge of procuring and would be discharged by the bench on the understanding that he would be sent to a corrective institution in west London which specialized in curing young boys of perverted desires.

And so the boy found a dungeon even deeper and danker than Brighton. The boy was stripped and shown homosexual pornography. If he responded with arousal, he was beaten. It reminded him of a story he had heard about the Gestapo. The Gestapo would strip prisoners naked, sit them down and run a live electric current a couple of inches above their crotches. Then they would bring into the room a beautiful Jewish woman who would strip in front of them. The prisoners had been without sex for years in some cases. They could not control or inhibit their bodies, they were driven mad with a desire they knew would kill them. Afterwards, as the stripper put her clothes back on and they dragged the bodies out by their feet, there was the stench of singed flesh and shit. Sometimes, before

134

the woman put her clothes back on, in a windowless room full of freshly dead bodies and smelling of shit and burned flesh, the guards would rape her, one after the other. The boy thought about this, decided he was better off, as they would never actually kill him. And then sometimes, as the days stretched into weeks, he wished they would kill him. They called it aversion therapy.

At night, the staff who took off his clothes during the day, and brought the visual material, and slapped him about, these same staff took off his clothes in the dark, and caressed him, and slapped him about, and held him down so they could take him, one after the other. He bled and ached, constantly. Then one day he got hold of some pills and tried to kill himself. He awoke in the hospital wing and wondered momentarily if this were it, heaven, the other side, eternal life for ever and ever, amen.

His eyes saw white light with a cross in the middle. He clenched them shut. The light hurt his eyes, reached into his brain and hurt that too. Would his head ache like this for ever, then? Would it hurt for ever when he went to the toilet? Would he *need* to go to the toilet? He opened his eyes and the white light and the cross sharpened, came into focus, as he blinked, and he realized he was looking at a window. The white light was the sky above the Goldhawk Road. The cross was the frame of the window. So it was a kind of heaven after all, or at least a future. It was a window on the rest of his life.

He looked around. A couple of other people lay sleeping beneath stiff blue blankets. He smelled Dettol. He sat up, dressed hurriedly from the pile of clothes in the bedside locker – grey trousers, grey T-shirt, plimsolls. His own beautiful clothes, his drape jacket and belted raincoat, his trousers with knife-edge creases, his drip-dry, slim-fit shirts, his real leather shoes with metal toe- and heelclips, were locked up elsewhere and would be sacrificed to the escape, the flight from the past. He threw up the sash, climbed through the window and dropped fifteen feet into an alleyway, making no sound in his plimsolls. Then he walked off towards Shepherd's Bush and into the rest of his life.

For several years he did not go back to Brighton. He stayed in London, but on the other side, Mile End way. He learned a trade, and he learned to have sex with lovers rather than punters. He went to drag shows – plenty of those for such a rough, butch neighbourhood. He drank and forgot. For days on end he forgot, but then a memory crept up behind him, tapped him on the shoulder and walloped him between the eyes when he looked round. He learned to ride these blows, to bob his head around them. He discovered he was good with money, good at making and saving it. He bought property and traded up. He met people who went to Brighton at weekends.

Some of them followed drag artists who performed down there, some just went for the change of scene. It was very butch and gangsterish, Mile End way, and the boy couldn't be doing with it. So why didn't he come to Brighton? He'd like it in Brighton, he really would. Very jolly, and the salt was good for your pores, just don't get it you-know-where. But the boy always declined.

Then he got some news. His sole remaining contact with his family was an older sister who rang him occasionally. She rang to say his father had died, accident at sea. The boy silently exulted, standing there holding the receiver, winding the cord tight round his finger. He did not go to the funeral, he did not talk to his mother, who had played the radio so loud. He bided his time and when he got the all clear from his sister – the family house was sold, his mother had moved – he laid his plans.

Where he had seen shadows and a fist, now he saw light and caresses. Someone said to him, when he moved back to Brighton, 'You'll love it here. When I've been away and I come back over those Downs and see the streets spread out over the hillsides, when I see the piers and smell the sea, when I get blown by the wind in those streets down to the sea, I think I've come home to the lost fucking tribe.'

And Graham said: 'Buy me a drink before I fucking weep.'

Chapter Eight

Biding my time on the seafront I fell into an arcade of old slot machines. To make them work you bought a stack of old pennies: five for 50p, filthy with age, poor old ramrod-backed Britannia matt with dead skin and verdigris. I rested my forehead in the worn brass eyepiece of What the Parlourmaid Did, and cranked the handle. The effect was unexpectedly erotic.

You had to squint to catch the flickering kinematic image. It took time for your eyes to adjust to the dim light, to rationalize the strangely three-dimensional effect. You might have been kneeling to peer through a keyhole, you felt like a voyeur, which was partly what gave the experience its strange erotic charge. What the parlourmaid did was to shed her clothes whilst sitting on a divan. You saw her from behind the divan, the back of her head encased in a tight bob, as she performed this sedentary striptease. A leg shot out, from which the parlourmaid unpeeled a stocking; then the other leg. An arm held out a corset, suspended from one lacy-gloved finger, which dropped to the floor; then a bodice; finally the lacy gloves.

At this point, when she may be imagined sitting naked on the divan, though one saw only the tight bob and the slender, naked nape of neck, a man appeared in the frame from the left. The man was you, the onlooker; or rather, he was the person the onlooker wished to be at that moment, the person about to ravish the naked and compliant parlourmaid. The man in the frame acknowledged his other, excluded self by looking over towards the eyepiece/keyhole and winking. He then flung himself on to the divan, the bobbed head fell from view, the film ended, and imagination supplied the rest.

As well as merely watching, the onlooker could control the parlourmaid, bend her to his libidinous will, for he dictated the speed at which she moved. If he cranked the handle fast, her striptease was perfunctory, unexciting; but if he slowed it down, the tension built, the erotic charge intensified to a most uncomfortable and delicious pitch. The appearance of the man, the moment when he flung himself on the divan, was the moment of release. It was advisable to stand cross-legged whilst enjoying the venereal pleasures of What the Parlourmaid Did. All for 1d!

I had three turns with the parlourmaid, playing her like a fish on a line, slow, quick, slow. After the third go, an obscure drizzle of self-loathing seeped into my soul and I determined to spend the last 2d on more innocent pursuits. So I posted one of the pennies in the slot of the Spiritualist Room.

This was a sitting room in which two women were sitting facing each other across a table covered in a black cloth, their hands resting on the edge of the table. A dog lay on a circular rug in front of the fireplace above which, oddly, hung a portrait of Benito Mussolini. A bookcase and a tall cupboard completed the furniture in the room. As the penny dropped a ceiling light came on and the two women, rather alarmingly, came to life, both moving slightly, in ways that suggested adjusting their seating positions or making themselves more comfortable. Nothing happened after that for a couple of seconds or so.

The black cloth on the table implied a seance and I filled those moments with incantations and voices from the grave. The seance was evidently successful in summoning spirits, for soon the fun began. The table rose and hovered, pitching the women back in their chairs, as if in amazement. The rug with the dog lying on it spun like a top, Mussolini turned through ninety degrees, the bookcase wobbled, the door of the cupboard opened and a skeleton popped out. Operated by near-invisible wires, the skeleton performed a sort of jig in front of the two ladies. Still leaning back in their chairs, they looked suitably awestruck. I had to show Roger the Spiritualist Room. He would love it.

We had arranged to meet on the Lower Esplanade between the piers. After the inconclusive meeting with the sensitives Roger had been put off the idea of paranormal exploration of the origins of the Shakespeare portrait. 'I don't mean to be rude,' he had said to Flo, 'but it just doesn't work for me.' Flo had agreed that that was his prerogative, and she understood how he felt, but perhaps he ought to give it one more go. You got bad mediums just as you got butter-fingered glaziers or unsympathetic doctors. The thing to do was to shop around until you found one you liked and trusted.

Flo suggested Roger attend a spiritualist church just off the Western Road. The medium who regularly took services there was highly thought of and had a particular interest in psychic painting – pictorial renderings of the spirit world by people who had passed over, using mediums to do the drawing or painting – so he might feel a certain affinity with the Shake-speare portrait. Roger still wasn't convinced but I had per-suaded him to follow Flo's advice, which was why the previous Sunday he and I were to be seen filing into a bungalow annexe off a narrow twitten joining the Western Road with Lands-downe Road, on the borders of Brighton and Hove.

Roger wanted out as soon as we were inside. But the row we had chosen to sit in, one from the back, had already filled up, making it awkward to leave, and besides, I felt that having come this far we should see it through. There was something creepy about this freshly done bungaloid extension with Artex ceiling and melamine altar, something sinister in the juxtaposi-tion of home improvements and the shadow world. The people were odd too, in their sheer democratic variety. I had expected the dippy and the desperate, New Agers with rings through their tongues, tribal chants in their hearts and crystals in their pockets; old biddies wearing bicycle clips and bifocals. Instead the thirty or so people in the hall struck me as a pretty fair cross-section, the kind of sample you might get in the queue for a cashpoint or an ice-cream. This was disconcerting. Their ordinariness raised the possibility that many more people were walking around harbouring beliefs in the spirit world, in the possibility and the wisdom of communing with the dead, than you had thought.

For half an hour the service more or less ran on traditional lines – hymn, prayer, reading, hymn, address. Sitting on my plastic chair behind half a dozen rows of entirely sane-looking necks, my attention began to wander to the bookcase on the wall beside Roger. I nudged him, directed his gaze to *Psychical Experiences of a Musician* by Florizel von Reuter and *Medium* by Ena Twigg. We sniggered silently at each other's shoes. The officiating medium, the one Flo had suggested might be our man, wore a blazer and red tie but in other respects seemed pretty much like a vicar. He had a round face, as if someone had drawn the outline from a dinner plate; he smiled with unflinching benignity, made a steeple of his fingers and spoke lispingly in cotton-wool platitudes about God and love.

But then suddenly, like some awful, snazzy lager commercial, Derek Nimmo became Christopher Lee as he narrowed his eyes and invoked the power of 'the Great White Spirit'. From this point the service parted company with conventional Christian liturgy. This was the bit people had been waiting for. Derek Nimmo stood on the dais, clenched his eyes tight shut and swayed slightly as if falling into a trance. Then he opened his eyes wide and scanned the rows of expectant faces. Again I had the uncomfortable sensation that the psychic could look into minds, that he would peer into mine and see foolish scepticism there. He spoke like the host of a television discussion programme. 'You, yes, the lady in the green top, third row.'

He beamed at her. 'Just behind you, I'm seeing a tall man with thinning hair. Am I right?'

'Bless you,' she said. 'Yes, bless you.'

'He thinks you've been worrying too much lately about little things. He wants to tell you not to worry any more. He says you've always taken the weight of the world on your shoulders. He wants to tell you to relax and enjoy life. Life is a wonderful gift. Am I coming through?'

'Yes,' she said. 'Oh yes. Bless you.'

Derek cracked a big smile. 'And now,' he said, 'he is holding out his hand. Just by your right shoulder. He wants to comfort you. Can you feel him? Extend your right hand. There. Do you feel him?'

'Yes,' she said. 'Yes yes yes.'

Roger and I remained pretty much unmoved by this. The idea that someone took life too seriously, was continually anxious for the well-being of their fellow-man, even to the neglect of their own interests, was a piece of gross flattery to which most people would succumb. But Derek was just warming up.

He spent some minutes feeling his way into his next subject, opening and closing his eyes, looking puzzled, studying the rows of expectant faces. Finally he pointed to an empty seat between two women and said, 'I'm not sure which of you two ladies this applies to, but I'm getting a large nappy pin . . .' The women looked at each other and shook their heads. 'Is there a baby, a baby who perhaps didn't remain very long on the earth plane?' The women shook their heads again, and a susurrus of embarrassment passed round the congregation. 'I'm sorry,' he said. 'I'm still getting this nappy pin. It won't go away. At least, it's a large pin, a large safety pin. Presumably for a nappy.'

And then one of the women shrieked. 'A kilt! A pin for a kilt! Yes, bless you, bless you!'

We had an argument about this later. Roger said that Derek might have heard the woman speaking with the trace of a Scots accent. I pointed out that only the Anglo-toff type of Scot, the public-school, rugby-playing solicitor type, ever wore kilts nowadays, and anyway her accent was pure Estuarine. We also argued about what happened next. Derek began to act as if his feet were stuck fast in quick-drying cement, trying in vain to tug his feet from the boards of the dais.

'I'm getting badly damaged feet,' he said. 'I can't move the feet. There's a bad injury, or an accident perhaps.' The woman nodded vigorously, pathetically grateful, and the congregation murmured with amazement.

I thought for a moment he meant stigmata, that so divinely favoured was the kilted spirit that he had taken on the marks of crucifixion in his feet. But Derek had not gone that far. Evidently this was a literal injury suffered by the woman's loved one whilst still on earth. She didn't specify what the injury might have been, beyond the fact that it was both feet at the same time. But, again, it was a wildly speculative and risky choice on Derek's part if he were merely an ingenious fraudster. Why choose an injury to both feet – surely pretty unusual – when you could play safe and opt for a stroke or heart attack? This convinced me that Derek was worth approaching with the Shakespeare portrait. Roger still wasn't keen but at the end of the service I insisted we wait and talk to Derek anyway, see what he said.

The congregation filed away until there were just a couple of old ladies stacking hymnbooks and straightening chairs. Derek had retreated to a back room. I pushed the door and it swung open to reveal Derek slumped in a chair with tie loosened, looking exhausted. He raised a glass of water to us and said, 'Thirsty work.' Between us Roger and I told the story of the portrait and wondered whether he would help.

Derek Nimmo cleared his throat and said, 'Forgive me. One of you thinks I'm a fraud, and the other isn't sure, though I can't tell you which is which just at the moment – the batteries are running a bit flat. I felt you out there, during the service.

143

Am I right?' We looked at each other and shrugged, feeling his eyes on us. 'I'm sorry,' he said. 'I don't waste my time trying to help people who won't help themselves.'

When Roger arrived on the Lower Esplanade I took him to the old amusement arcade and spent my last 1d showing him the Spiritualist Room. The joke fell a bit flat. Roger had been hoping he could dispense once and for all with the psychic angle, by finding conclusive academic evidence on the origins of the picture. That morning he had set off for London with high hopes. He had an appointment with a man called Rolf Popp at Sotheby's who had sounded enthusiastic on the telephone, confident he could help.

Popp's initial reaction had been promising, Roger said. In principle, yes, it could well be of Shakespeare, in the sense that it was certainly in the style of the late sixteenth century; he thought it might well be Dutch. He had then taken it upstairs to the print department, and when he returned he seemed much less enthusiastic. The experts upstairs had confirmed it as a nineteenth-century lithographic print and put a value on it of less than £100. As requested, Roger had also brought along the tatty old frame in which he had found the picture in Balchin's junk shop. Rolf Popp found a code number stamped on the back, 46 SMV, which he recognized as a stamp from rival auction house Christie's. Obligingly, Popp had phoned Christie's. He was told that the picture had been presented to Christie's in 1961 by a collector in Brighton, but had been turned down as unsaleable. While he remained courteous, Rolf Popp's attitude was now different from when Roger had walked in. Popp thought he had found pearl, but it was only grit after all. 'Shit!' Roger suddenly thumped the venerable old cabinet containing the Spiritualist Room, and the portrait of Mussolini fell from the wall.

'Let's go,' I advised Roger, steering him to the door. Outside I tried to cheer him with the prospect of the walk I planned to take him on, to Rottingdean and back along the Undercliff. When you communed with the sea, it put life in perspective. When you saw the sea's power, you realized how puny were your own flappings of desire, your thwarted dreams. Meeting the sea now and again, as far as possible on its own terms, was salutary. 'Come on,' I said. 'Let's blow all the shit away.'

This was not so immediately possible. The sense of the sea's savagery was all but lost in Brighton amid the ribbon development along the coast. It was possible on a blustery day to stand on the seafront and watch a storm, be thrilled by its power, but it was from a position of relative safety, with buildings immediately behind you, in the knowledge of warm, dry places close by. The weather in Brighton was not savage, as a rule. If you wanted coastal frenzy you needed to go east.

Eastward, from the Marina to Rottingdean, was a coastal footpath of two miles on which it was impossible to hide from the anger of the sea. The Undercliff path was built in the Depression years of the 1930s, largely by the unemployed of Brighton and out-of-work miners from the coalfields of the north and of south Wales. It was part of a general development of the coastline which also included the construction of the clifftop road, Marine Drive. At intervals of half a mile there were steep flights of steps linking the path with the road above. In between, the sea had you in a room with the door bolted behind it.

There was a wall, shin high, between you and the narrow strip of beach. On the landward side the base of the cliff had been reinforced to a height of about fifteen feet with a sloping stone buttress. But the significant point was, you could not retreat from the sea beyond the width of the path until you came to one of the flights of steps. The sea demanded your constant attention, commanded that respect be paid. Every year people died for being insufficiently respectful, every year people ventured on to the Undercliff when they shouldn't.

That morning when I woke and looked from my attic windows I saw the grey Channel angry and raw with broken water, heard the wind shaking the chimney pots of Brunswick Town, and thought: Let's do the Undercliff walk. I wanted to see the white frenzy of waves lashing against the low sea wall and being thrown upward in parabolic spouts by the wind; to hear the battering of the waves on the beach, the booming of the wind across the sea, to feel myself being jostled by the wind, ears aching and heart exulting with the wind.

There was another reason for wanting to do the walk. When Roy Boulting was reminiscing about the making of *Brighton Rock* in the long, hot summer of 1947, he told a story about the actress Hermione Baddeley, who played big and blowsy Ida Arnold. Hermione Baddeley had been good friends with another Hermione, actress Hermione Gingold. One evening Gingold had belted down the A23 in her MG to spend a drunken evening by the sea with Baddeley. They had started in the Grand, where cast and crew were based, and ended on a beach below the Undercliff path where they had drunk champagne and swum naked by moonlight.

The story came wrapped in a tissue of happiness – the champagne in the veins, the warm sea, the dancing fragments of the moon's reflection, the liquescent pools of silken underwear on the pebbles. And then two teacherly trouts from Roedean School appeared, apparently out of nowhere, screamed with shock when they saw these strange, naked, swimming women, told them they were on school property (nonsense, of course). The Hermiones simply invited them into the water, but the mistresses turned and ran, disappearing as abruptly as they had materialized from the warm darkness. It was a theatrical happening, as if the Undercliff path had become a stage with wings and trapdoors for sudden entrances and exits. Where had they come from, and returned to? The problem was solved when Baddeley found a heavy steel door recessed into the brick buttress which shored up the cliff face: a tunnel!

I was intrigued by the notion. Imagine a subterranean passageway linking Roedean School, the Colditz on the cliffs above, with the beach. Redolent of smuggling and sex, the idea had the ring of myth about it – assignations between posh gels in gymslips and wiry old salts smelling of herring and baccy; lesbian orgies by moonlight; solitary suicides and third-form pashes. When you looked at the height of the cliffs, and the distance of the school, you reckoned that sinking a tunnel would have been a complicated, ambitious undertaking. With what purpose in mind? Imagine though, twenty-odd years ago, if we had arrived for our Christmas disco out of the ground, like an invasion force, retaining the element of surprise! The tunnel was a Freudian kind of wishful thinking, no more.

But then someone else assured me the tunnel really existed. This was the mother of a work colleague, whose first teaching job, in the early 1960s, had been at Roedean. She remembered the tunnel, she said, because at intervals on the walls there had been alarm buttons with a sign attached: IN CASE OF FIRE OR MEN, RING ALARM.

I checked with the school direct, expecting suspicion if not hostility. Why would a strange man want to know about a subterranean means of access to a girls-only boarding school? Writing a book, indeed! But the woman who answered the phone was charming and brisk. 'Oh yes,' she said. 'There's a tunnel. Starts by the main gate. Kept locked at both ends, of course. Used by the gels when they go on field trips by the seashore. Inspecting rocks and seaweed, that sort of thing.'

Her response, the alacrity with which she had yielded up the information, had been disappointing. I wanted the tunnel to be apocryphal, or, at the very least, to be a closely guarded secret. I didn't like this prosaic, A-to-B sort of tunnel, this let's-go-for-a-nature-ramble business. Part of the reason for the walk to Rottingdean was to uncover evidence for the tunnel at the appropriate point, below the school, on the Undercliff – a door or gate, or a bricked-up section of wall. And if I did find the entrance to the tunnel, it would be a doorway on desire, it would be *my* tunnel, not the real one.

I had a call to make before we set off. The little fishing museum was near the penny arcade, and the curator, Mike Strong, had become a friend during my time in Brighton. I intended just saying hello, but Mike was in talkative mood. The previous week I had asked him about murders in Brighton, and there was one he had forgotten to tell me about. 'Back there,' he said. 'There's his picture.'

Mike pointed to a painting hanging on the back wall of the museum, of 'Captain' Fred Collins. I had heard of Collins. When he died in 1912, at the age of eighty, practically the whole of the town turned out for his funeral. He was a fisherman who showed the way by diversifying into pleasure boating, and was skipper of the famous Brighton tripper boat the *Skylark*, the first of successive generations of boats of that name in Brighton. It seemed that, in every Edwardian photograph of the beach, the *Skylark* insinuated itself in somewhere.

Collins was a 'character' who had his fingers in many Brighton pies. Never seen without his shiny black waterproof hat, he hung out in the pub he owned, the Fortune of War in the seafront arches, where he sang songs and told stories. Collins had a son, also called Fred, and between them they had the seafront businesses – fishing, pleasure boating, bathing machines, fishmongery and ale – sewn up. One evening in the Fortune of War there was a disagreement between the Collinses and a man who was drunk. Father and son sorted it out emphatically by killing the man, though they never faced charges. In all the eulogies and tributes which followed the senior Collins's death, this incident was not mentioned.

Roger and I set off for Rottingdean with the wind parting our hair, and talked of meteorology. Roger said things could get quite wild enough without having to walk the Undercliff. He remembered, with a druggy clarity, a day and night of high winds which had turned Sillwood Place into a scene from nightmare.

Few of his neighbours remembered this, perhaps because it had been over Christmas and the largely flat-dwelling population of the area had been spending the holiday in houses, well away from the mayhem. Things got particularly bad because the frontages of the surrounding buildings happened to be undergoing a paint job and were covered in scaffolding. Residents had been furious that the painting had not been completed as scheduled, because it meant the scaffolding being in place when many residents would be away, giving easy access to empty flats. Roger, however, fancying a seaside Christmas for once, had invited his brother down.

When his brother arrived in the early afternoon of Christmas Eve he had remarked casually, 'Bit blowy out there,' and they had thought nothing more of it as they drank lager into the twilight and reminisced about awful family Christmases past. By six o'clock they were ready to continue their drinking in a pub, but when they reached the entrance of the building on the ground floor they were unable to get out as the wind had created a vacuum between the inside and outside doors. At first this seemed like a huge joke. Already half-cut, they took it in turns to try tugging the inner door open, then tried both together, standing one behind the other like a pantomime horse, before collapsing in giggles.

Then they noticed what was going on outside. The wind was trapped and snarling in the small square, violent as a cornered lioness. It swirled around the square, looking for a way out, it jack-knifed, it pushed against the invisible forcefield of isobars that imprisoned the coast but, finding no escape over the sea, continued its circling and prowling with renewed ferocity. It wailed and moaned in great anger and pain, it shook the embroidery of scaffolding on the front of the houses and tossed scaffolding poles into the air as if they were matchsticks. The poles bounced and clanged along the streets, sending up sparks, deadly as shrapnel. Not a soul walked abroad.

Roger and his brother stared open mouthed at this spectacle. But there was no question of them remaining inside. Christmas had to be toasted in appropriate fashion, come what may, and so they resumed their struggle with the vacuum-sealed door and finally, in a lull of the gale, they broke the seal, forced open the inner door and found themselves out in the street, sheltering their heads and looking fearfully around.

Roger had had a particular pub in mind, but the wind did not care to allow them there. Instead he decided simply to follow the wind and keep moving – for to stop was to be blown over or have a scaff pole or roof tile crack your skull – and trust that sooner or later a pub would present itself. In the end they saw a door with a brass plate and etched-glass panel in it and aimed for it. A foot or so from the door the wind lifted them from behind and hurled them into the bar so that their feet barely touched the lino. It was like arriving in an unfamiliar time zone in a science fiction story. The door banged closed behind them; the silence of the bar seemed deafening after the murderous rushing outside.

They looked around, cautiously, expecting scores of eyes to be upon them, expecting laughter and funny hats and Christmas cheer. But the bar was empty, on both sides. Ashtrays were freshly wiped; there were full bowls of peanuts, crisps and cubes of cheese on the top of the bar. But actual drinkers, or staff, there were none. They called behind the bar, they waited, one of them went upstairs and knocked on doors there. No answer. They looked at their watches, they waited some more, they looked at their watches again.They shrugged their shoulders, went behind the bar and helped themselves.

They had another. Even after forty minutes, when they were on their third, they expected the barman or landlord to appear with an explanation for his absence, connected to the weather. But the barman never did appear. An hour and a half later, they left the bar as they had entered it, in a great spurt of wind. The bowls of nibbles on the bar top were badly depleted. Thoughtfully placed on a towel between the pumps were two used pint jugs, rimmed with foam, and two spirit glasses. Otherwise you would never have known.

'And the funny thing is, you know,' Roger yelled above the sound of the wind as we approached the Undercliff path, 'the funny thing is, I'm not sure which pub it was now. Everything looked so different when things were back to normal.'

Today's wind was nothing like as fierce, yet it shook a loud, sporadic applause from the rigging of the yachts in the Marina basin. Just beyond the hideous neo-Georgian waterfront villas and the vulgar, blue-windowed cruisers, the Undercliff path started. 'Are you sure you want to risk it?' asked Roger. The sea was breaking high above the low wall and hurling itself at the base of the cliffs. But we agreed we were not in the mood to turn back.

The cliffs curved here so that we could not see very far in either direction. Together with the restrictive visibility of the sea fret this produced a sense of isolation, of walking but not getting anywhere. To the landward side the cliffs towered oppressively; on the other side – beyond the path, the wall and the ribbon of shingle beach – was an unimaginable volume of water. Steering between these uncountable tonnages of rock and sea, with the waves threatening to batter you to oblivion, you felt the elation of the person with nothing to lose.

We watched the waves as we walked, trying to gauge the big ones. The low sea wall checked the progress of the big waves, but did not stop them altogether. Instead, with a thunderous clap, the water shot up vertically, twenty, thirty, forty feet in the air, falling in a lace curtain of foam, soaking the path, turning it into a quagmire. But then, every so often, a wave was too powerful to be sent completely vertical by the sea wall; instead it continued its forward momentum, merely scudding over the wall, hitting the cliffs and bouncing back

151

into the cycle of things. And these were the dangerous waves, the ones that threatened to carry you off. It wasn't even a case of anticipating these whoppers and taking evasive action, for there was nothing to be done, no handles to hold on to, nowhere to hide. If the wrong wave should come along, it was tough. Still, we found ourselves hugging the cliff wall as we walked, and clinging on to each other's shoulders when a big one looked to be on its way.

The idea of a tunnel, or at least a door in the cliff wall behind which one might find sanctuary in a storm, made more sense than ever now. From looking at the map, I calculated we must be drawing in line with Roedean School, high above us on that lip of greenery that sloped down to the cliffs. We began to watch for a likely-looking doorway, and soon enough we found one. It was recessed at an angle into the sloping wall which buttressed the cliffs. At the back of the doorway was a heavy, rusty steel door. The door was fixed closed by means of heavy bolts that did not look as if they had been drawn for a long time. We huddled in the doorway, looking in vain for something with which to attempt to prize open the door. Then we gave up and enjoyed the relative protection the doorway afforded from the wind and water.

I tried hard to imagine opening the door and seeing the two Hermiones cavorting naked in the moonlight on a summer evening fifty years ago. But the images would not form. Below the sea wall, where their underwear had pooled over the pebbles, a dark, round object was being washed back and forth in the frenzy of foam. I thought suddenly of the head a man had reported seeing at Black Rock, just the other side of the Marina; a head, if head it had been, which had possibly belonged to the unknown victim of the First Brighton Trunk Murder. Was I too seeing a severed head? It was the size of a head; it seemed to have hair. Thin strands of hair were visible, waving in the foam! With heart thumping, with a sense of both dread and shameful elation, I shot from the doorway, ignoring the waves raining down, for a better look. It was – oh joy, oh shit – a large coconut.

The weather got worse, rain slanted in off the Channel, visibility dropped to a few yards. The walk was no longer enjoyable. We pressed on at near-jogging pace till we reached the steps which took us up to Rottingdean. We found an old pub in the High Street, the Black Horse, which had sunk below the level of the road so you had to bend and duck to get inside. I had fancied a drink in the White Horse, on the cliffs, in remembrance of a hilarious story I had heard about the landlord of this pub and Rudyard Kipling. But the original White Horse had been knocked down and replaced with an unpleasant-looking lager palace so we passed on it.

In the snug of the Black Horse we bought drinks and I told Roger the Kipling story. Kipling had moved to Rottingdean, to a house called The Elms, on The Green, in 1897 and lived there for five years. Though still in his thirties the author of *Kim*, the *Just So Stories* and patriotic verses on the Boer War was a famous national figure. The landlord of the White Horse, Stephen Welfare, who ran a horse-drawn bus service to bring trippers up from Brighton, hit on the idea of laying on detours to Kipling's house. It was a handy way of stealing a march on his rivals in the highly competitive tourist bus business: 'Come to sunny Rottingdean and see the soldiers' poet AT NO EXTRA CHARGE'.

Picking up his customers in the Old Steine, Welfare advised them to ride on the upper deck of the open-topped bus, for the walls surrounding The Elms were high (Kipling valued his privacy). The first Kipling knew of this enterprising little venture was when he was sitting in his garden reading the day before's *Times* one Sunday morning and he looked up to see a row of people grinning at him like monkeys from above the garden wall. 'An' 'ere we 'ave Mr Kiplin', the soldiers' poet,' shouted Stephen Welfare triumphantly, gesturing over the wall at the astonished writer. Kipling began to wave his newspaper

153

back and forth as if swatting flies. The effect was so unintentionally comic that the rubberneckers on the bus roared with laughter. Here was Mr Kipling, large as life, looking – there was no doubt – precisely as Mr Kipling should look, in cream summer suit, with panama hat, those distinctive round spectacles, and yet here he was also acting like a cartoon come to life, as if he were on a verandah in the Raj. Where were the punka-wallahs?

The sightseeing visits quickly became popular, and Kipling went ballistic. He talked to the local constabulary, who told him that Mr Welfare was not actually committing an offence. He tried reasoning with Welfare face-to-face, shouting at him with as much politeness as he could muster over the garden wall. 'Respect, Mr Kiplin',' Welfare yelled back, 'a man's gotta make a livin'.' Kipling was becoming a prisoner in his own home, frightened to set foot in his garden for fear of being ogled. The buses might turn up at any time of day, any day of the week.

Unable to heed his own injunction in his most famous poem about keeping one's head while all around are losing theirs, Kipling sat down and wrote a pleading letter, appealing to the man's better nature, and posted it off to the White Horse. Welfare was delighted by the letter. He took it with him on his next bus trip to The Elms. ' 'Ere we 'ave the splendid abode of Mr Kiplin', the soldiers' poet – observe the great man peeping from yonder window – and *'ere'* – he waved aloft the letter – 'we 'ave a missive, written and signed by the great man himself, in that very abode, only yesterday. What am I bid for this rare and gen-wine artefact? Do I hear five shillin's . . . ?'

Kipling hared downstairs and out into the garden. 'Mr Welfare,' he yelled, trying desperately to keep the lid on his rage, 'did you not receive my letter?' A buzz of excitement passed around the top of the bus at the sight of Kipling the Writer Fellow at such close quarters. Evidently, too, he was on close terms with their driver and guide.

With his pith-helmeted patriotism, his gung-ho verses and mass popularity, Kipling was a very un-Brightonian sort of writer. In the Black Horse, as Roger and I sat there drinking and laughing at the notion of Kipling blowing his top, I spotted a reminder of his diametric opposite, the quintessence of writerly Brighton. On the wall next to the public telephone was a poster advertising a production of 'Patrick Hamilton's gripping Victorian thriller "Gaslight", with Louise English (from TV's "Brushstrokes")' at a theatre in Eastbourne.

Gaslight was a conventional if clever melodrama which found wider fame via two feature-film versions in the 1940s and 1950s. The commercial success of *Gaslight*, and of another play, *Rope*, which Alfred Hitchcock made into a film, enabled Hamilton to keep himself in finely tailored suits, hand-made shirts and great lakes of alcohol; and, when he wasn't incapacitated by drink, to continue writing weird, funny and dark novels. I had just finished reading *Hangover Square*, a sublimely titled prose poem of infatuation, despair, madness, alcoholism and murder set in the sleazy purlieus of Earls Court and Brighton.

Patrick Hamilton had been an unholy mess of man, a gentleman who haunted dive bars and cheap boarding houses, a Marxist who became a Tory, a vituperative bore and a braggart, a drunken, chain-smoking wreck – a true Brightonian, as Kipling could never have been.

The weather was foul when Roger and I left the Black Horse so we caught a bus into Brighton and walked along the seafront back to Sillwood Place. In the hallway we took off our soaking waterproofs, and while Roger made tea and crumpets I sat in an armchair next to a bookcase. I then did what I often did in the vicinity of a bookcase – I put out a hand and without looking picked a book at random. The book I picked was a biography of Patrick Hamilton, *Through a Glass Darkly* by Nigel Jones.

This seemed strange enough, given the conversation we had just had about Kipling and Hamilton. But then I opened the book and started reading. Patrick was a small child living in First Avenue, Hove, shortly after the turn of the century. One of his treats was being allowed to help the cook, Mrs Collins, known as Collie Dog, make toffee and soda cakes. Another was listening to the tall tales of nautical derring-do spun by Mrs Collins's husband, 'Captain' Collins, skipper of the pleasure boat *Skylark* and proprietor of the Fortune of War pub down in the seafront arches, who got away with murder.

Chapter Nine

I was living by a gathering place of ghosts, a psychic fault-line. Right outside Fredda's house the pavement changed, York stone to the west abutting cheap pink concrete to the east, signifying the border between Hove and Brighton. Here, at night, as I watched from the sky, lonely strangers came from east and west to seek love and orgasms. Here, too, you might see the spectres of the Boulting Brothers in knickerbockers, escorted by their nanny, executing a smart about-turn as they approached the invisible but impenetrable wall between Hove and Sin City; or Daisy Noakes, the blind nonagenarian, miraculously nine again, approaching from the other side and peering with both wonder and distaste at the poshness and presumption of Hove. 'Hove, *actually*', Brightonians called it, in sarky reply to the imaginary question, 'Oh, you live in Brighton, do you?'

Things happened at this border. One December evening a good seventy years ago, Mr Graham Greene walked this way, and settled in a seafront shelter just down there. With a promising first novel under his belt, and having made the decision to resign his job-for-life as a sub-editor on *The Times*, Greene was just getting used to the idea of spending his future being A Writer. It was a cold, bright night and, gazing seaward, Greene noted, with the forensic precision he was learning to cultivate, how the thin line of the surf appeared phosphorescent in the moonlight and how the frosty wind smoothed off its rough top edge.

So preoccupied was he in registering these observations that he had not noticed that the shelter had another occupant. Suddenly a voice from the far corner said: 'Do you know who I am?'

Greene started and peered into the shadows. He could barely make out a human form, let alone recognize it. 'Er, I'm afraid I don't,' he said politely.

'I'm Old Moore,' said the voice, meaning of *Almanac* fame, the anonymous astrologer whose predictions are published every year. Failing to understand the reference, Greene said nothing. 'I live alone in a basement,' the voice continued. Greene still said nothing, wondering what he could possibly say to this rambling, lonely old geezer. 'I bake my own bread.' The silence lengthened, intensified. The sea made little rushes on the beach. The voice resumed. 'The *Almanac*, you know,' it said humbly, realizing the young man hadn't understood who he was. 'I write the *Almanac*.'

Old Moore, the voice from the shadows, found an immortality in the booklets bearing his name. But Greene perpetuated him in another way, by turning him into the bent, broken lawyer Prewitt in *Brighton Rock*. Greene conjured a whole life, or rather a death in the midst of life, from that voice in the seafront shelter where Brighton runs up against Hove. Racked by a stomach ulcer, married to a hag with a passion for tinned salmon, lusting after typists, Prewitt fights urges to expose himself in a public park. '"This",' he says, quoting from *Dr Faustus*, '"is Hell, nor are we out of it."'

Greene wrote that 'poor, hopeless Mr Prewitt' was the only character in the book that had sprung from his actual experience of Brighton. The rest of the book, he said, was the invention of the characters he himself had originally invented. *Brighton Rock* was a fiction twice over, funnelling back into the shadowy seafront shelters of the imagination. Greene's Brighton was a state of mind.

Like the Boultings, Graham Greene saw his first film in

Brighton, at the Savoy Cinema just round the corner from the Star and Garter/Dr Brighton's. The film Greene saw, a silent one, was called *Sophie of Kravonia*, about a kitchenmaid who became a queen, a 'high romantic tale, capturing us in youth with hopes that prove illusions, to which we return again in age in order to escape the sad reality'. Kravonia was 'the area of infinite possibility' and *Brighton Rock*, he said, a very poor substitute for it – 'like all my books, and yet perhaps it is one of the best I ever wrote'.

I found out much about the Brighton of Greene's novel from a native New Yorker and adoptive Brightonian called Maire McQueeney, who first showed up in the town assuming there was an offshore promontory called Brighton Rock. Now she ran a *Brighton Rock* tour, among other literary walks and outings around Sussex. I joined one of the tours on, appropriately enough, the former Whitsun weekend, which is when the novel opens. We met outside the station, which is *where* the novel opens, with the holiday crowds that came in by train from Victoria every five minutes, and Maire wore a cream-coloured, circular, cotton sailor's cap of the sort sold on the Palace Pier in the 1930s.

Here we all were, enough of us to form a razor gang, feeling suddenly like extras in the fiction. We walked down Queen's Road, where the holiday crowds rocked, 'standing on the tops of the little local trams, stepped off in bewildered multitudes into fresh and glittering air', then sloped off left to Tidy Street, two lines of low old terraces with basements which matched the locale of Prewitt's miserable abode, 'in a street parallel to the railway beyond the terminus'. Maire subtitled her tour 'A Seaside Excursion to Hell and Peacehaven', the latter being the eastern clifftop suburb where the drama of the book reaches its climax. From Tidy Street we walked down to The Level and boarded a coach there, sped up Elm Grove, past the racecourse, cut back through Whitehawk, past the kind of neat, barren, bourgeois roads where Pinkie hid after being razored on the racecourse, to Marine Parade, and on past Roedean, and Rottingdean's pipe-dream villas, to Peacehaven.

Built after the First World War and very nearly called New Anzac, Peacehaven was designed by an American architect, which accounted for its grid system of roads – like New Jersey, said Maire. On top of the cliffs, streets still ended in obscurity, in a pool of water and salty grass. Rain was falling, a filthy night, when Pinkie drove Rose out here so she could shoot herself through the ear, 50 per cent of a suicide pact he had no intention of completing. A radio played, and in a garage a man was doing something to his motorbike which roared and spluttered in the darkness.

Now it was Sunday morning, fine and blowy up on top of the cliffs, and men in the identically sized realms of their bungalows were still filling up the hours against eternity, vacuuming car boots, levering earth from their golf spikes. Here Rose was saved and Pinkie went over the edge. They couldn't even hear a splash, says the book. I looked over, saw rocks and pebbles. It would have been more like a *splat*. Maire said: 'People who don't belong are the whole world, according to Graham Greene. Being a Brightonian is the nearest you'll get to being an insider.'

Brighton Rock was up for grabs. Even Greene did not lay claim to it, admitting the novel had been hijacked by its characters. Yet there was a topographic exactitude to the book. You could walk down the steps at the base of the Palace Pier to the scene of Fred's murder. The old Bedford Hotel, which burned down in 1964, was the model for the Cosmopolitan, where the mobster Colleoni lived – 'where did you bring a swell blonde to if not to the Cosmopolitan, coming down by Pullman at the weekend, driving over the downs in a scarlet roadster?' Frank's place, where Pinkie and the gang lived and Spicer died, was number 63 Montpelier Road, and so on. I enjoyed wandering Maire's version of *Brighton Rock*, but I also looked forward to creating my own.

The time for this was later in the summer, when I noticed a poster on the seafront advertising several days of race meetings at Whitehawk. The racecourse was Brighton's pathological side. There was a story I heard repeated several times, always about different Brighton pubs. A mobster pays a visit to a landlord who has stopped paying him protection money. He doesn't slash him with a razor, as Pinkie does to Brewer. He carries a sports bag, which he unzips. He pulls out a carrier bag, hoists it on to the bar, grunting slightly under its weight, and invites the landlord to look inside. The landlord pushes down the sides of the bag to reveal what looks like the top of a plum pudding. Puzzled, he peels the bag back further and realizes he is looking at a swollen, battered, bloody severed head. 'Meet Sam "The Man" Maloney – the last geezer who had the bright idea of stopping paying his protection money,' says the mobster. 'Say "gottle of gear", Sam.'

In every case the person who told me had been told by someone else, had not actually seen it for themselves. Details varied, of course, but the essence of the story remained the same. Brightonians were proud of the story, it was part of the self-mythology of the place. If you messed with the main men down here you got heavy shit. It had started with the race gangs in the twenties and thirties, everyone knew that. Brighton then had been crawling with Al Capone types in baggy pinstripes and pencil moustaches. Just like William Hartnell in the film *Brighton Rock*. Any self-respecting Brightonian knew that.

But Brightonians sometimes didn't know as much as they thought. One Thursday night I had gone to the Grand Hotel and sat in the pillared bar feeling tiny as a child in a cathedral. A cocktail pianist in a white tux was tinkling away – Jerome Kern, Cole Porter, and Gershwin of course. A drunken wedding party had limped on into the evening and their laughing and shouting drowned out the piano for all but the odd note or phrase, yet the pianist carried on regardless, massaging the keys

161

and rolling his shoulders. When it came to his break I invited him over for a drink.

Harry Arnold was eighty-four and remembered Brighton in the bad old thirties, the time of the race gangs. He went to Sherry's dance hall then, paid 6d to sit in the balcony and watch Mancini, the Italian mobster, and his cronies, milling about below. 'I think you mean Sabini,' I said. 'Mancini was the chap who got off the Trunk Murder.' But Harry was insistent, and who knows, perhaps he wasn't so wrong. (To complicate matters, at least one anthologized account of the Brighton Trunk Murders claims that Toni Mancini had worked for a London gangster named 'Harry Boy' Sabini before moving down to Brighton.)

The truth was that there wasn't a dominant gang in Brighton, contrary to Greene and general assumption, though there were various small outfits. Sabini had been a criminal of the time, though not particularly associated with Brighton, and there was no evidence that he had a penthouse suite at the Metropole, the Bedford or anywhere else. He may have been the gang leader whose anonymity Greene was careful to keep in his autobiographical collection of essays *Ways of Escape*, who retired to 'a gracious Catholic life in one of the Brighton crescents', or he may not.

What seemed clear was that Harry, and Roy Boulting, and anyone else of that era, had long ago absorbed the rumour of mafia carry-ons and Al Capone-type big cheeses, of wide lapels and thin moustaches, to the point where it had hardened into self-evident fact. There were no mobsters and molls in the Grand that Thursday, just a straggle of golf club drunks from Steyning or Burgess Hill with carnations in their buttonholes and sex on their minds. Harry sat down and played for them, 'Someone to Watch Over Me', and not a blessed one of them heard.

Brighton was never as violent as it liked to think. Between 1930 and 1939 there were only seven murders in the town, only three successfully prosecuted cases of extortion, twenty-nine of grievous bodily harm and seventy-one of prostitution. Hardly heavy shit. The race gang trial of 1936 in Lewes, which Greene claimed broke the Brighton gangs for ever, was in fact of a London gang called the Hoxton Mob – sixteen of them received sentences averaging twenty-seven years for attacking a bookie called Solomon and his clerk at Lewes racetrack.

The effect of banging up the Hoxton Mob was certainly to clean up Brighton races – but no more than Goodwood, Lewes or any racetrack in the south of England. Lewes, in fact, was a more violent racetrack than Brighton, but Brighton needed the aggravation and spinsterly Lewes most certainly didn't. So Brighton took the coshes, razors, iron bars and snarling intimidation off Lewes's hands, and mythologized itself as a Chicago-by-Sea. As Auden said, if you expel the devils you run the risk of expelling the angels along with them. Brighton needed its devils to ensure its angels stayed put.

Greene did his bit. Although he admitted he had met only one gangster who could have belonged to Pinkie's gang – 'a man from Wandsworth dog-tracks whose face had been carved because he was suspected of grassing to the bogies after a killing at the stadium' – he drew on the very few real Brightonian murders of the era to set the tone of menace. Hale's murder, he said, was based on the kidnapping of a man on the seafront whose body was found 'out towards the Downs flung from a car'. The killing of Pinkie's mentor, Kite, before the book starts, in the waiting room at St Pancras Station, has echoes of the First Brighton Trunk Murder in 1934, in which the legs belonging to the torso found at Brighton Station were discovered a day later in a suitcase at King's Cross.

Greene makes up a murder too. When Pinkie goes to Rose's house in Nelson Place he sees an old newspaper on the step bearing the photograph of a young girl called Violet Crow, 'violated and buried under the West Pier in 1936'. There is no record of any episode remotely resembling this, though the name Violet Crow might have been taken from the name of the victim of the second Trunk Murder, Violette Kaye.

We've reached deep into Greeneland by this point. The borders are unpatrolled and the place teems with chancers, with both real people and fictional characters staking claims to the meaning of his books. One of the writer's recent biographers has even commandeered a battered old suitcase full of supposition and faulty logic on which to stand and accuse Greene of committing the First Brighton Trunk Murder. (He adduces Greene's alleged misogyny, his dreams of committing murder, alleged clues in various texts, particularly *Brighton Rock* itself, and so on; which merely goes to show that Greene, like Shakespeare, is who you want him to be.)

Here's a punt of my own. In the course of researching murders in the town I had unearthed a cracking killing from about the right time which may well have given Greene a crucial part of the plot of *Brighton Rock*. This killing took place in October 1936, the trial in December, a good eighteen months before the publication of *Brighton Rock*. The case was widely reported and so voluptuously Brightonian it seems unlikely Greene would have failed to spot it. An added kick, from my point of view, was that it had happened in Brunswick Terrace, at number 33.

Here, in a two-bedroom flat, lived a middle-aged bounder called Arthur Cyril Jefferson Peake, on the proceeds of a £600 annual allowance he received from his wealthy estranged wife. Described as a former army officer, set designer, art collector, boxing promoter and flower-shop proprietor (what an accretion of wastrel occupations!), Peake was in the happy position of not having to work for a living. Indeed, his allowance was enough for him to support what is described in court cases as an extravagant lifestyle.

He even employed a 'chauffeur-companion', called Arthur Geoffrey Noyce, whom Peake occasionally passed off as his son.

This relationship, between a rich roué who had left his wife, and a fair-haired, penniless and uneducated twenty-one-year-old boy, was described by prosecuting counsel as 'a friendship much stronger than that existing as a rule between employer and employed'. Neither in the court proceedings nor in newspaper reports was the relationship ever explicitly said to be homosexual.

One October evening Noyce left the house he shared with his mother in Meeting House Lane and walked to Peake's flat for dinner. The electricity had failed so they ate by candlelight with the gas fire providing an additional, comforting orange glow. Afterwards they played draughts.

Next morning, the maid smelled gas coming from the apartment and rushed upstairs. She found Peake slumped by the gas fire. The gas tap had been tied in the open position with a sash cord. Peake was unconscious, face down towards the fire. Ann fumbled with the knot tying the cord, turned off the gas and opened the window. As she turned Peake over on to his back she noticed there were superficial slashes on his wrists and around his throat. Then she turned to the bed and saw Noyce lying there beneath a blanket. He had a sash cord wound round his neck and he was dead.

Peake was charged with murder and the trial opened at Lewes Assizes on 9 December 1936, just five months after the trial of the Hoxton Mob race gang in the same courtroom. Peake's defence was conducted by Norman Birkett, who two years earlier had successfully defended Toni Mancini in the Brighton Trunk Murder Case. Peake claimed that he had popped out to make a phone call to his sister, and when he got back he found Noyce sitting in the armchair foaming at the mouth with the cord round his neck. Evidently he had tried to commit suicide by self-strangulation during the few minutes that Peake was out. Peake had put Noyce to bed but he had not recovered.

Bereft and deranged, and believing he would be accused of

murdering Noyce, Peake had then attempted suicide by gassing, but not before writing this cleverly self-serving note which was read out in court to the all-male jury: 'How can I explain this? I left Arthur when I went to phone and when I returned I found him with a cord round his neck. I tried to bring him back but it was too late. I had told him what my wife had said about him but I did not think he would take it like this. I am taking my own life. I cannot face this. I have been slowly murdered by my own wife, and this poor boy is another victim.'

A doctor from Hove testified that, while self-strangulation was theoretically possible, by tightening a ligature oneself from the front, in this case the signs were that the cord had been tightened from the back, by someone else. Famous Home Office pathologist Dr Bernard Spilsbury (whose career, incidentally, Greene followed with interest) went further. At the scene of the crime, he sat in the armchair in which Noyce had supposedly strangled himself and tried to do likewise.

He survived to testify at Peake's trial that in his opinion self-strangulation was not possible. How seriously he had tried to prove otherwise would never be known.

In his summing-up the presiding judge, Mr Justice McKinnon, directed the jury to consider what the verdict would have been if Peake had succeeded in gassing himself. The conclusion, he said, would have been that Noyce and Peake had died in a suicide pact, and indeed much of the evidence suggested this might have been the case. But as it was the law, in those days, that the survivor of a suicide pact was always, automatically, found guilty of murder, Peake had had to pretend that Noyce had killed himself out of the blue. Hence Peake's suicide note followed by his rather unconvincing attempt to kill himself. Peake was found guilty of murdering Noyce and sentenced to death by hanging. Three days before sentence was carried out he was reprieved and sent instead to Broadmoor.

In *Brighton Rock*, Pinkie persuades Rose to agree to a suicide pact, with no intention, of course, of carrying out his half of the deal. He must make it look as if Rose killed herself after he had threatened to leave her, for a verdict that she died as the result of a suicide pact would send him to jail, or to the gallows. After they are married, after they have consummated the marriage between two clangs of the doorbell, with one of the swiftest, least believable acts of intercourse in literature (Leonard Bast's impregnation of Helen Schlegel in *Howard's End* runs it close), Rose leaves a token of love in Pinkie's pocket.

It is a note written in a big, unformed hand: 'I love you, Pinkie. I don't care what you do. I love you for ever. You've been good to me. Wherever you go, I'll go too.' Disgusted by its sentimentality, Pinkie is about to throw it in a dustbin outside a fishmonger's when he realizes it might be useful one day. The suicide pact idea has not come to him at this point, but when it does the note assumes significance. Sitting in the hotel in Peacehaven before they drive out to the cliffs, supposedly to kill themselves, Pinkie produces the note and a pencil and tells Rose to add a line to it: 'Say you couldn't live without me, something like that.' He explains: 'This is a pact. You read about them in the newspapers.'

The conventional wisdom about *Brighton Rock*, encouraged by Greene himself, is that it is an unbalanced novel. 'The first 50 pages ... are all that remain of the detective story,' he wrote. What followed was a drama designed to show up the distinction between good and evil, right and wrong. But the background of that drama is still a trashy world of sensation and tabloid journalese, of love songs, advertising slogans, sex manuals and scandals in the *News of the World*, that looks remarkably familiar, sixty years on. The case of Jefferson Peake and Arthur Noyce has the ring of one of the stories dropped into the novel for background effect, like 'Woman Found Drowned at Black Rock' or 'Assault on Schoolgirl in Epping Forest'. But it's a reasonable hunch – especially given the timing of the case and Greene's familiarity with the careers of Bernard Spilsbury and Norman Birkett – that the Noyce murder is more substantially present, living on in the clever suicide pact story thought up by Pinkie as a way of getting rid of Rose.

Greene went to the races in August 1936, shortly after reading the newspaper reports of the Hoxton Mob trial at Lewes Assizes. He wrote to his brother Hugh in a state of anticipation and excitement, asking if he and his wife wanted to come along: 'I wonder if you and Helga feel inclined for a day of low sport . . . I warn you that I shall want to spend my time in the lowest enclosure.' I said something similar to Roger, who said he was feeling lucky. I was, at last, entering my own *Brighton Rock*.

I got the street map out. I had decided, as far as possible, to walk everywhere during my stay in Brighton. It saved money, but it also brought the place alive, made you look up and down, from the soles of feet on attic balconies to bald spots in basements. To get to the races Roger and I would go via the parish church of St Nicholas – a fragment, a haiku of old Bright-helmstone. It was a foggy, humid morning that might hold in store either rain or blazing sunshine. The low, lopsided church, on a grassy hill on the edge of the old town, materialized slowly through the mist. Paths fanned through the graveyard, which is full of mossy headstones with weather-worn inscriptions. One commemorates Phoebe Hessell, who died in 1821 at the age of 107, had nine children and served for many years as an infantryman in the British Army. As an old crone she sat at the corner of the Old Steine and Marine Parade selling gingerbread, pincushions and trinkets and showing people her bayonet wounds. How on earth, in more than twenty years, was she never exposed as a woman by her fellow-squaddies? Because, presumably, they never held urinating competitions and never washed. It didn't bear thinking about.

As Roger and I paused for a breather at the top of the church-yard we noticed three people processing solemnly in a line between the headstones, looking ethereal in the mist. They held divining rods, which twitched as they walked. 'We're mapping the underground streams,' said one. 'There's a concentration of ley lines under here and they produce the streams.' I remarked that in general the churchyard was probably a good place to find energy sources, having been here a long time, and it had probably been a site of pagan worship and burial even before that, etc., etc. He looked unimpressed. The girl with him, who wore a hood and pale make-up so she looked like a witch, said: 'Shoreham's better. There's a trans-dimensional gate in Shoreham cemetery.'

We dropped down to the east of the railway station, an area of land, like many adjacent to railway property, discarded like carpet off-cuts. The bricks were blackened and the buddleia sprouted, waving purple fronds in the still, moist air. St Bartholomew's Church, the notorious brick Noah's Ark, was somewhere around here.

Anglo-Catholic St Bart's, taller than Westminster Abbey, was built a hundred years ago. Cheese warehouse, people called it, brick Noah's Ark, brick parallelogram, Popish Trojan horse. The Noah's Ark insult stuck, and people Chinese-whispered it into fact: the conspiracy of High Church clerics responsible for St Bart's had taken the mythic dimensions of the Ark, measured in cubits, and turned them into bricks and mortar: making whoopee with the Good Book. (This was demonstrable rubbish, as the dimensions of the Ark in cubits translated as 450 feet long by 75 feet wide by 45 feet high, more like an Asda superstore than a church. But it was a good story.)

Once, hovels had clustered at its base as medieval slums had clung to Chartres. Now, the new buildings surrounding it compromised its height so you rarely got the full effect. But then, walking alongside a line of houses with ramps for wheelchairs, suddenly the façade seemed to drop from a great height as if unrolled from the skies. The brick was shocking, like a pedestrian precinct standing on its end. A vicar beckoned us in with an encouraging smile.

St Bart's was an oddball sort of place. Designed as a sort of

Gothic basilica, with no aisles and no apse, no spire or tower, it looked rather obscenely naked from the outside, like a hairy dog after a bath. Inside, you couldn't decide whether you were in Italy or Russia, or perhaps Greece, for it looked half Orthodox, half Catholic, but never what it was, which was good old, vapid old you-put-it-on-hospital-forms-after-scratching-your-head-for-a-second-or-two C of E. Over the altar was a towering Byzantine baldachino of marble, gold mosaic and mother-of-pearl; the font was of green marble, the pulpit of green marble supported on pillars of red marble. The acrid, decadent whiff of incense hung in the air, a smell that, not being a Catholic, I still associate with the kind of college girl who liked Jefferson Airplane and knew how to put on a condom with one hand in the dark. This was a bells-and-smells sort of high church with knobs on. Round the walls were curious confessional boxes, of glossy polished wood with sky-blue velvet curtains.

Confessionals in the Church of England? A rather camp young vicar grinned and bobbed and agreed it was unusual. 'Those boxes came over on the back of a ship all the way from Russia. Imagine!' And he made big saucer eyes at us. But were they used? Did people clamber into them and admit – what? What did people confess to in confession? He said they were scarcely used; he made a joke of it: 'Because there are no sinners in this house.'

Not fancying the hill of Elm Grove, we took a bus to the racecourse, past the palmist and the betting shops. The mist had not burned off, as we had expected, but closed in. At the top of Elm Grove it was wet and corrosive, making us cough slightly, like the stuff you get on top of mountains. The mist separated the track from the houses, flats and churches and returned it to its former, annexed state. Here Regency swells with thick heads had grown drunk all over again, this time on unaccustomed draughts of upland air. Here the Hoxton Mob, or was it the Sabini gang?, had traced the shape of hatchets beneath their coats as they waited at the turnstiles.

This was Brighton's back yard, away from prying women's eyes, a man's domain, nicotined and desperate. Up here, above the damp tenements, far away from the sooty basements of old London, with all that air giving you an extra 10 per cent, things became possible to a man.

There was no sign of Greene's 'plebeian procession' to the racecourse. No one got off the bus with us at the top. Perhaps I had got the wrong day – but there were the cars on the sloping field of the car park, like toys on a cushion. Racing usually attracted fuck-off motors, big silver Mercs and Range Rovers with bull bars. There weren't many about today, just the odd personalized number plate. Otherwise it was small men's cars with coathangers for radio aerials and *Dalton's Weekly* in the back window.

We went in the Paddock for £4. What a placid mob! Men with aubergine faces beneath tweed titfers milled contentedly from Tote window to bar to course-side bookies. The odd yuppie type in mail-order shirt swilled lager and munched spicy hot American chilli dogs from a steaming kiosk. Expecting summer sun rather than this clammy mist, everyone was underdressed. They turned their collars up, stamped their feet and grinned ruefully at one another. Roger nudged me and produced a hip flask of whisky from his coat.

There was a shambling pace to proceedings, as if real life was too frantic and fast and it could damned well wait for once. The course commentator had that honeyed toff's voice that has something of the quality of lullaby. After the first race, the Kemp Town Maiden Stakes, he said: 'The stewards decided that Little Fizz interfered with Mrs Middle at around the two furlong mark, but as both were unplaced the result stands.'

The bookies were magnificent, exotic creatures, like Wild West physicians, like characters out of Graham Greene. Theirs was a silent, mime world. The latest odds tick-tacked back and forth between the rows of bookies in the Paddock and their counterparts in the Enclosure. They stood on milking stools in

171

front of a board of runners and as they received new information they continually rubbed out and updated the odds.

Some wore fingerless gloves, like entrants in a Fagin looka-like competition. Gladstone bags full of money hung open on hooks behind them. They had made an effort, Sam Trumpton of Eastleigh, Bob Murphy of Chertsey, Bob Tell of Hither Green, *et al.*, to look like the kind of men you would be happy to enter into financial arrangements with. They wore suits and ties and periodically produced combs to lick their hair back into place. But gremlins had got into their wardrobe. They wore their calling on the outside.

It wasn't just the fingerless gloves. One wore black shoes with sparkling toecaps of a different colour, ruby red; another had a shoe with the sole hanging by a thread, lolling like a tongue as he shifted position on his milking stool; a third had the screw top of a half-bottle of whisky protruding from his jacket pocket. They smoked, cupping their hands over the cigarettes like Private Walker in *Dad's Army*.

Two things everyone knew about Brighton racetrack were that it was a linear track – an inverted U, in fact looking from the south – and that it was council-owned and run, making it a democratic, class-blind sort of place. Proscribed by its white rails, it disappeared into the misty distance, starting to curve before it fell completely out of view. In the crook of this curve, as if hugged by a friendly arm, rose the blocks of flats of the Whitehawk estate. As the afternoon wore on and the mist grew thicker, these flats vanished completely and the commentator had problems till the horses were coming off the bend.

I put £2 on Sooty Tern to win in the 3.45 Eric Simms Memorial Handicap at four to one. The jockey was called Royston Ffrench. I wondered whether this spelling was simply a typo in the race card but no, it was repeated on another page. I reckoned any horse ridden by a man who sounded as if he wore cricket flannels and a monocle deserved my money. Roger put the same amount on Apollo Red at five to two, on the grounds that he was owned and trained in Brighton and might be expected to feel at home; also, he was ridden by a woman called Candy Morris, which sounded like the name of a sex therapist.

The horses cantered up and down, their rumps like polished conkers, their hoofs on the turf making the air tremble. Royston looked magnificent, tight as a spring, in his silks of lavender and black hoops. The horses dematerialized in the mist on their way to the start. The odds on Sooty Tern had lengthened slightly to nine to two.

The commentator was at sea until the final three furlongs. I trained my binoculars down the track and slowly the bunch of runners and riders hardened from the whiteness into a silent, smoking coalescence. Sooty Tern did not feature in the commentary. 'And it's Night Wink on the near side by half a length from Victory Team with Apollo Red gaining on the rail, it's Night Wink, it's Night Wink . . .' The turf beneath our feet began to shake. Now I could differentiate the jockeys' colours. Lavender-and-black was not in the leading bunch, was nowhere to be seen – and then I saw it, at about the same time as the commentator: 'And with a furlong to go Sooty Tern is coming on the outside, it's Sooty Tern . . .'

Roger offered the hip flask again. I tilted it and gasped. The commentator bellowed in amazement at the audacious run Sooty and Royston conjured from way back in the field. Sooty's nostrils looked like portholes as he flashed past. Royston's colours were bright as a maharajah's in the afternoon gloom. They moved together like an oiled machine, crossed the line a length clear of the field. Yes!

I joined the queue for Sam Trumpton of Eastleigh, the one with the whisky bottle in his pocket, handed him my red and yellow numbered ticket, and he dipped his hand in his leather bag and handed me back a tenner. Turning to Bob from Hither Green he said, 'I'm going to where the money is next week. Kempton Park and fuck this.'

In the Racehorse Inn, half-way down Elm Grove, Roger and I drank London Pride on the winnings, sitting next to a man wearing white shoes and a hairpiece. Riah by Fludes.

Chapter Ten

One Monday in July it rained and rained in Brighton. The rain turned the three attic windows into portholes of frosted glass. The rain gurgled in unseen drainpipes and blanked out the sea. The few people who moved on the seafront wore brightly coloured rain gear and half trotted. The Meeting Place was a sorry sight, forlornly leaking steam from its beverage-making machines and with not a customer all afternoon. There was no escaping that this was a day to write. On a fine day, of sun and promise and blithe girls, I could be out there on the seafront lapping it all up, and still be working. I could clench shut my eyes to register the effect – a brass band mauling Scott Joplin somewhere far away, the tomfoolery of the rollercoaster on the Palace Pier as it writes its letter O in the sky, the orange contagion of sun on the eyelids. But today was the lonely slog.

I stood at one of the rainy windows and phoned Maire McQueeney. I had some query or other, I forget precisely what, on Greene and Brighton. She answered my question soon enough and we got into a general chat. Did I have a title for the book? she wanted to know.

Breakfast in Brighton, I told her. 'It's named after a painting.'

'Oh. Who by?'

'Someone called Edward le Bas.'

There was a pause. 'It's funny you should say that . . .' replied Maire slowly.

Maire had cornered the market in literary and artistic walks in Sussex. She offered, for instance, 'Eric Gill's Ditchling', and 'Virginia Woolf's Lewes', and also compiled companion booklets for the walks. One of these booklets had found its way to an antiquarian bookshop in Bloomsbury, where, the week before, it had been picked up, pored over and finally purchased by a couple of American lesbian professors of English literature at a university in the Midwest. Patty and Fay were on a literary pilgrimage of England. They had been to the Lakes of the Romantics, Bram Stoker's Whitby, the Hay-worth of the Brawn-tays, the Naddinghamshire of Lawrence and the Hampshire of Arse-tin. But they had left the best, the most personally resonant and psychically significant, till the final few days of the trip: the Bloomsbury group and, in particular, of course, Virginia Woolf.

Browsing in this old bookshop in Bloomsbury itself, just by the British Museum, and coming across these nicely turned-out booklets on Virginia Woolf's Sussex, they took them back to the hotel and called the number listed at the bottom. Relieved to be talking to a fellow-American after having just tried in vain to order cold beers in a pub off the Tottenham Court Road, they put a proposition to Maire. Would she customize a day out for them around Lewes, taking in the sights associated with Virginia Woolf?

A deal was struck. Maire had arranged to pick them up from Lewes Station the day after next. The day's excursion would include Charleston farmhouse and the house at Rodmell where Virginia and Leonard Woolf were living when Virginia committed suicide. It would also take in – and this was the interesting bit, said Maire – the tiny church at Berwick whose walls were hung with murals painted mainly by Duncan Grant, with help from Vanessa and Quentin Bell and Anjelica Garnett. These murals included a very large, dramatic rendering of Christ on the cross by Duncan Grant, known as *The Victory of Calvary*. The model for Christ in this painting was Edward le Bas. Would

I, asked Maire, like to come on the tour with Patty and Fay, see the painting for myself?

Despite his love affair with the half-Japanese concert pianist, Miyadera Schwabe, Edward was predominantly homosexual. If he is remembered at all now, it is as a minor twinkle in the Bloomsbury firmament. I knew of his friendship with Duncan Grant and Vanessa Bell, but didn't know about the painting in Berwick Church until Maire told me. Edward met Duncan and Vanessa in the early war years, put Duncan up in his house in Bedford Square, hosted foreign trips to Venice, Padua, Castelfranco, Asolo, Lucca, Siena and Pisa, to Tenerife and to Marbella, where he bought a house. Edward even played a part in the meeting between Duncan and the beautiful young Paul Roche in 1946.

It was an extraordinary, hilarious encounter. Ever on the lookout for young talent, Duncan noticed a sexy sailor boy waiting to cross the road at Piccadilly Circus. He spoke to him and invited him, then and there, back to Edward's house in Bedford Square, where they drank rum. Duncan fell in love, discussed Roche exhaustively with Edward, and was only moderately put out to discover, several weeks later, that Roche was not a teenager but thirty, not a matelot but a Catholic priest. Still, these were mere details, and they remained close for the next thirty years.

From the little I had read and heard about Edward le Bas, he seemed to have been that rare thing, a person without side: genuine, entertaining, kind, witty and empathetic. Charles Lamb had been like that, so they said. Michael Palin was, nowadays. Edward was known, but never *well* known. When he died, in the New Forest in 1966, his obituary in the *Daily Telegraph* was the size of a small ad for a holiday cottage in Devon. He generally earned an inch or so of entries in the indexes of the biographies of Bloomsbury types. In one biography of Vanessa Bell he had come across as particularly diffident and effete, to the anger of his family.

Edward's niece, Jennifer Pearse, wrote me several letters about him. Her mother Mollie was Edward's sister. 'My mother, who was very close to her brother, was upset by the rather feeble picture it [the Vanessa Bell biography] gave of a most unfeeble person!' she wrote.

Perhaps the problem, for a writer, is that niceness is difficult to characterize without it sounding like blandness. Jennifer managed to convey something of his spirit, though, in one special memory of her Uncle Edward during his *Breakfast in Brighton* period:

> He painted a portrait of me in 1956 in the studio he had built over the garage at No3 Vine Place, just behind Clifton Terrace – or rather he wanted to paint a chair and needed someone to sit in it – or so he said. He was always the greatest fun to be with and a great giggler. I don't know how the portrait ever came to be finished but each time I look at it, it reminds me of him and of very happy days.

Reappraising Edward's life in a small-circulation art magazine, the director of the Tate Gallery, Sir John Rothenstein, declared that 'he was so modest that he detested personal publicity and accordingly his own painting never received the recognition it merited'. However, Sir John stands on his own foot rather by then banging on about Edward's worth as a collector, as a generous bequeather of art to public galleries – not least to Sir John's own Tate – for the encouragement and help he gave to other artists, and as a fine human being, whilst skating over his painterly accomplishments, and not even mentioning *Breakfast in Brighton*. Sir John concludes with a vague hope that some day Edward 'will be accorded an honoured place in the history of twentieth century English painting – one which he never expected'.

I fancied – piecing together fragments about the man – that

Edward had been his own accomplishment, that it was his life, rather than the body of work he produced during it, that was the work of art. *Breakfast in Brighton* was no great shakes in an art-historical, aesthetic sense – the woman I spoke to at the Brighton Art Gallery had said it was 'nice enough, but not a significant work'. Yet it immediately meant a great deal to me, as if it had bided its time, waiting for forty-odd years for the person to come along who spoke the same language. This is a terribly solipsistic view, of course, as it is a very accessible painting and no doubt many people have fallen for it (including the competition entrant who sent in the postcard to the newspaper I work for). Still, like a charming host – like, by all accounts, Edward himself – that was how the painting made you feel, as if you were the sole beneficiary of its attentions and charms.

Getting to know the painting, meeting it, as it were, in the flesh, I reckoned I was becoming acquainted with Edward, too. He may have been born in London and died in Hampshire, and lived here, there and everywhere as well as Brighton, but Edward was above all a Brightonian. Glamorous, louche, effortlessly talented and modest to a fault, like the first, fattest, campest, most dyspeptic Brightonian of the lot, the Prince Regent, Edward had made living art of his time by the sea.

I had seen his self-portrait at Mr Warren's, and one rather fuzzy group photograph taken in northern France in which Edward appears alongside Clive and Vanessa Bell and Duncan Grant, with a wispy beard that looks French-bohemian, but I didn't feel I had the measure of how he had really looked from these images. The prospect of seeing Duncan Grant's Edward/ Christ was intriguing. And the idea of Edward posing as Christ in the first place was a huge joke. Delusions of parity with the son of God were the mark of invincible megalomania, of genocidal despots. Yet here the role was filled by a fastidious epicure, a man remarkable for his love of paintings and wines, his modesty and self-deprecation. The occasions on which he posed for Grant for the Berwick Church mural must have been strange and amusing.

As arranged, Patty and Fay were waiting outside Lewes railway station. Lewes is Brighton's spinsterish elder sister, the kind of person Brighton could have been if only she had gone to church and preserved her virginity. A bloke who drank in the Grosvenor had a barber's shop in Lewes. Though he toned down his campness when he was working in the shop, his sexual orientation was still pretty obvious. Yet he reckoned his customers didn't have a clue. They wouldn't recognize a homosexual if one pronged them from behind while they were brushing cut grass from their Hush Puppies, because men who fancied other men didn't exist in their scheme of things. Not to exist was worse, in fact, than being hated for being a poofter. The short back-and-sides merchants of Lewes, said the barber, were brain-dead.

A woman called Kelly who went in the Grosvenor, bought her clothes in fetish shops and wore panda eyes of mascara, had a similar story about Cornwall, where she had grown up. When she was seventeen she went to France with her boyfriend and once they were there they decided they didn't want to go back. For three years they moved from country to country in Europe, earning money by busking in squares and on street corners. He played a penny whistle and she tap-danced. They acquired a small dog who danced too. Then they split up and she moved back to Cornwall.

On her first night back she went into the pub she had drunk in as a teenager. A few contemporaries from secondary school were in, playing pool as they had been when she left; the barman was the same, except his sideburns were greyer. They looked at Kelly as she walked in and murmured, 'Hello, Kell,' then resumed what they had been doing. After three years! Maddened beyond endurance by this, Kelly caught a coach out of Cornwall the next day. She went first to London, then to

Brighton, because someone at a party in a squat in Turnpike Lane told her the clubbing scene there was ace. She had been in Brighton ever since and said she would never go back to Cornwall.

I remembered walking through Lewes ten years before with an old girlfriend. She was just telling me that she had known someone from Lewes at university who had inherited a lot of money and never had to work, when she broke off and said, 'My God, there he is!' Across the road, a Wodehousean cove in tennis whites ambled along, pinging a racquet against his knees as he went. She called out his name and waved. He stopped and looked, stooping and squinting like an old man though he couldn't have been more than thirty. 'Ah, hello,' he said finally. 'Jane.' He pointed his tennis racquet along the street. 'Anyway, must . . .' He didn't finish the sentence, but implied pressing business and ambled on his way. Jane and I stood dumbfounded, watching him go, then laughed. 'Imagine living here!' we said. What it must do to your brain. Outside London and Brighton, England was like those old sods in the barber's in Lewes: brain-dead.

Yet the dessicated old bird that was Lewes had some racy stuff in the cupboard. Lewes was built on a steep ridge above the River Ouse. The fabric of the town – its old brick, flint, timbers, tiles, weatherboards and mossy cobbles – had mellowed into tasteful autumn hues betokening continuity and stability. It had expensive antique shops and decent old boozers, not to mention Harvey's Brewery, which supplied its excellent bitter to the Grosvenor. On Sundays, when the rest of the universe was offloading cash at Asda or B&Q, scarcely a soul stirred among its twisting alleyways and steep streets. The last thing you might expect, in such a place, was the flourishing of independent thought. Yet Tom Paine, the radical political visionary, had lived here in the eighteenth century and written *The Rights of Man*, advocating votes for all, old-age pensions and free state education – dangerously sensible stuff, for which he was indicted for treason and had to escape to France.

Though we met Patty and Fay at the railway station, they had not come directly from London that morning but stayed overnight in a bed-and-breakfast in Lewes. Breakfast had been unbelievable – cold, rubbery toast; instant coffee; tinned orange juice, not fresh – and their room had been tiny, barely enough space between bed and wall to move in.

One was tempted to attribute this lack of space to the size of Fay's arse rather than the dimensions of the room. Fay was not fey. She wore faded blue Osh-Kosh dungarees and had a puddingy face and cropped hair so she looked like Andrea Dworkin, like a caricature of a lesbian. Patty, on the other hand, was rather frostily elegant in peach trouser suit, with wavy silvery hair and expensive-looking silver jewellery. She said, 'Oh my!' a lot, under her breath – not in an approving way, as Americans are supposed to do when gazing on half-timbered thatched cottages, but in a way expressive of disbelief and contempt. She would have said it when she and Fay were shown their room in the B&B, and when she raised the cup to her lips and tasted the breakfast coffee. She said it now in relation to Maire McQueeney's car. Maire drove a Mini Metro, crashing gleefully up and down the gears. With Fay and Patty installed in the back, Maire shot off into the Lewes one-way system. Fay's fingers closed on the back of my seat and Patty said, 'Oh *my!*'

One of the striking things about little Berwick Church was that the windows were of clear glass. The original windows had been shattered by a German bomb in 1944, shortly after the decorations of the church had been completed. They were replaced with clear glass to bring light to the new colour inside. The painting of the church walls revived a medieval tradition, though in fact the 'murals' in Berwick Church were done on boards, rather than directly on to the plaster.

The biblical scenes were mostly done in muted greens and browns, echoing the fields and woods surrounding the church.

But Duncan's *Victory of Calvary*, high on the west wall, featuring Edward le Bas as Christ on the cross, was done in vibrant post-Impressionist colours, with a bright blue cross against a vivid orange background. Edward faced slightly to his right, his eyes fixed on something far away, with a flimsy white wrap tied round his middle. Though he had nails in his hands and feet there was no blood; nor did he have a spear wound in his side. He would have been forty when Grant did the painting, yet he had the slender body of a teenager. Far from looking discomfited by the experience of crucifixion, he looked rather bored, which struck me as stylish and daring – of Edward to look like that in the first place, and of Duncan to render him thus.

Maire and I were sitting in the garden at Charleston drinking tea. Charleston was the farmhouse near Berwick Church, where the Bloomsbury lot had lived and loved and worked, painting the furniture whenever they were at a loose end (quite often, from the evidence). Duncan must have painted Edward here, in the studio within the house. Patty and Fay were on a guided tour of the house. I hadn't wanted to go on this tour – I had seen the house before – but I was interested in seeing the studio where Edward probably posed as Christ.

One of the Charleston guides had agreed to sneak me in for a quick look at the studio while the guided groups trudged from room to room. By a roundabout route, dodging in and out of doorways and rooms not on the official itinerary, we arrived in Vanessa Bell's bedroom. Here a door connected to the studio. While I stood by Vanessa's small bed and looked at her portraits of her sons Julian and Quentin, the guide opened the door a crack to see whether the studio was empty. A tour group was in there. The guide raised her finger to her lips and grinned, as if we were doing something illicit.

The guide checked the studio again, and beckoned me forward into the room. A door on the far side was closing as we entered, shutting out the murmur and shuffle of tourists. The guide whispered solemnly, as if to a visitor at a hospital bedside, 'I'll leave you alone for a few minutes.' I wasn't sure what she thought I wanted to do. I hardly knew myself, in any case. But I was glad she did leave me, because in the silence that followed a voice spoke.

The studio had colour-washed walls of pale blue and aubergine – pleasing, knocked-back shades. There were screens decorated with angular, flapper-era figures; a mantelpiece crammed with postcards, photographs, jars and bottles; a wood-burning stove whose base was inches deep in old cigarette butts; and an easel clenching a portrait in oils by Duncan of a naked Paul Roche. It was a cluttered room until the height of about eight feet from the floor. Then the colour and clutter stopped and it was pure, cool white, a trap for the light that flooded through the ceiling lights.

The voice said, 'Is that a bottle of *brandy* I see on the mantelpiece, Duncan?' The voice belonged to Edward. He was crucified on the easel. He stood on a low box. His ankles were tied loosely together with green garden twine. More twine tied his wrists to the cross-member of the easel. A piece of muslin covered his waist, knotted in a bunch at the side. In this position he could only see the mantelpiece by turning his head to the right and staring out of the corners of his eyes. 'I've been looking at it for the past hour and I've only just realized what it is!'

'Can you not look dolorous for just five minutes more, darling?' said Duncan Grant. He stood painting on a board propped against another easel. He wore a straw hat that looked as if it had been nested in by mice, and a tie held up his trousers. His nose, hands, shirt and trousers were spattered with orange and blue paint. 'Then you can have all the brandy you want. *Please* keep your head fairly straight on to me.'

'My trouble,' replied Edward, 'is I'm too good for this world. I want to be a bad lot again. Now, Duncan. *Please?*'

'On second thoughts, keep your head like that, tilted to the

184

right. That's it. Keep your eyes on that brandy bottle. In fact
– imagine you're drinking from it. With a fragrant cheroot on
the go . . .'

'Ahhhh,' said Edward. 'I must have died and gone to
heaven.'

Patty and Fay were getting into their stride now. In Berwick
Church they had been silent and diligent, taking photographs,
buying leaflets and postcards, accumulating material for future
seminars in the English faculty of Arkansas State University or
wherever they came from. Charleston, though, was more than
work. They emerged from the guided tour in a contemplative
state to join us among the hollyhocks in the garden. 'Probably,'
said Fay hopefully, 'Virginia Woolf would've sat here. Do you
think?' The 'Oh, my' as we kangarooed off in the Metro was
barely audible.

We went to Rodmell, now a dirt-rich hamlet between Lewes
and Newhaven lived in by television producers and inter-
national showjumpers. A cottage called Pear Tree Cottage had
a pear tree spreadeagled against it which looked like an
eighteenth-century botanical drawing. Here, in a higgledy-
piggledy house near the church called Monk's House, had lived
Virginia and Leonard Woolf. We poked around the tiny downstairs whose flagstones were cold even through leather soles.
In each room sat a volunteer steward who looked like Joyce
Grenfell. You could see down their schoolmistressy shirts but
didn't want to look. Patty and Fay burst from the house and
swarmed over the acres of lawn, hedge, pond and orchard.
Rolls of film bulged in the bib pocket of Fay's dungarees,
making her torso look carelessly sculpted.

On 28 March 1941, Virginia Woolf put on her fur coat and
boots and walked out through this garden and down to the
banks of the River Ouse beyond. Here she stooped to fill her
pockets with heavy stones. Then she jumped in the river. Fay
took endless pictures of the garden, as if Virginia's footsteps

might still be there, flattening the longish, lush July grass. The camera's motor drive whirred and the shutter clicked, and each time this happened, Patty finished her phrase: 'Oh my *gahd*, oh my *gahd* . . .'

Virginia Woolf's body was found in the river some days later. On his own, Leonard took the body to the Downs Crematorium in Brighton, and was horrified to receive Virginia's ashes back in a vulgarly ornate urn. He put her in a plain box before she was buried in the garden at Monk's House.

Virginia had started a roll-call of twentieth-century dudes who have been cremated in Brighton. It includes Vita Sackville West, Max Miller and Aleister Crowley, who died in Hastings in 1947. Crowley's followers conducted a black mass, amid the sylvan glades of Brighton's necropolis, as the Great Beast of Darkness burned off into the sky.

Patty and Fay lingered in the garden of Monk's House like lovers at a graveside. Perhaps, if they waited long enough, a tall figure in a fur coat would appear at the bottom of the garden, having changed her mind.

Chapter Eleven

I was late for an appointment in the Geese in Southover Street, a pub of crazed fiddle players and diminutive drunks. Brian Behan was installed in the corner when I arrived and on his second lager. Brian had a drinker's nose and spouted increasingly hilarious verbiage as he got tanked up. He even said 'beejasus' and 'begorrah', not in ironic send-up of himself but because these were the curses that fell naturally from his lips. Brian was a writer himself but he was known principally for being the younger brother of that legendary tearaway, drinker and playwright, Brendan.

I had first run into Brian in 1996. It was shortly before that year's arts festival and local television was filming part of a preview of the festival in an Irish pub called the Lion and Lobster. I happened to be drinking in the pub at the time and got roped in as an extra. The barman had just won an award for his cocktails. The idea was that he would rustle up his most lethal and garish concoction and slam it down in front of Brian, who was perched on a bar stool. The two would then run through a simple script which mentioned some of the highlights of the festival.

It sounded easy enough, but there were two problems. The first was that, though it was mid-afternoon, for reasons of atmosphere the scene had to look as if it was being filmed last thing at night (the barman even called last orders as he and Brian chatted). Curtains were closed, lights were dimmed, the hands of the clock were whizzed round to ten to eleven, and the few feckless layabouts who happened to be in there of a weekday afternoon were encouraged, in return for free drinks, to mill about in the background smoking furiously and looking the worse for wear. Why is it that when extras try to look like a crowd or a mob, a queue or a convivial gathering, they look like nothing on earth except, well, *extras*? The exasperated director instructed us to let our hair down more; he ordered more drinks, bought a packet of fags from the machine and passed it around. Then, as happy as he would ever be, he turned to Brian and the barman.

Here was the second problem. Brian insisted on tearing up the script. Or rather, like a greyhound chewing daisies when he is supposed to be after a mechanical rabbit, Brian ignored the script completely and went his own way. The barman would say, 'So tell me, Brian, are you going to be seeing any of the festival this year? I hear there's a fine line-up.' And Brian would reply, 'You know what, Dermot, I don't think I'll bother. It's all a load of gobshite anyway.' Or: 'Would you ever stop rabbiting on and make me that feckin' drink before I pass out.' This at least had the effect of solving the first problem – the whole pub was soon roaring and steaming. Each take necessitated Dermot making a fresh cocktail and soon Brian was well away. But, strangely enough, it was then that he began to talk sense.

Brian had talked about the sea. He had a friend from Saltdean who swam out and died. The cold acted as an anaesthetic, it was a pleasant way to end your life. 'I can't live without the sea,' said Brian, who swam in it every day. 'It's the father and mother of us all. It's an aphrodisiac, it increases longevity and improves circulation. You know, a group of Christians from the East End came down to Brighton, took twenty gallons of seawater back to Mile End? It's true.' He had even had a house on the sea. Living on a houseboat at Shoreham, Brian had been shot at, he said. 'They missed me. Oh, what the hell, that was all right, so long as they missed me.' At this point I think the director bought himself a drink and wrote the afternoon off like everyone else. I never saw the finished broadcast, but am told it was terrible.

On this occasion Brian was brimming with mirth. 'Would you look at that?' He threw a copy of that day's *Argus* at me. BRUSH WITH DEATH said the headline. *Teenager rescues fox after it falls 100ft from cliff.* I nodded and handed it back, puzzled – it was the kind of local newspaper story you get on a slow day for news. 'No, *look,*' he said. He prodded his finger at the top of the main photograph, where the photographer's name was credited: *Pictures: Brian Behan.* Brian had been cycling along the Undercliff, minding his own business, when, would you believe it, a fox came flying off the top of the cliff above and landed spreadeagled on the path in front of him. Telling the story, he opened one hand into a flying fox and bunched the other into a concrete path and effected a collision that nearly knocked our glasses over. 'I thought the focker was dead, of course,' he said. 'But no! It got up like a cartoon cat, shook itself as if it'd had a bit of a session the night before, and was off. *Vroom!* Straight in the sea.'

A young lad, Andrew Graves, who had been swimming on the beach, waded in after the fox, picked it up by the scruff of the neck and brought it back to safety. Brian had captured the moments of rescue with a disposable camera he had with him, and these were the pictures that now appeared in the local paper. There was also a quote from Brian, as given to *Argus* reporter Matthew James: 'It was marvellous. Andrew certainly saved the fox's life. He is a credit to his parents, his school and young people in general.' Brian was proud of the quote, the way it had struck exactly the right note. 'It just came into my head,' he said. 'What d'you think of it?' I said I thought it was very good. 'It's what people say, though, isn't it? You don't think I got carried away a bit when I said he was a credit to young people *in general*?'

Brian was tickled: here was a mad Irishman, brother of an even madder Mick, known to hold difficult views on society in general and the Irish Question in particular, who wrote plays about Islamic fundamentalism (and received death threats) and the British oppression of nationalist communities in Northern Ireland, whose word would normally stand not a cat in hell's chance of making the front page of a rag like the *Argus*; here he was, forming perfect tabloid soundbites and taking publishable, paparazzi-type tabloid pictures on his £4 throwaway camera. It was further proof that the world was constituted in the way that Brian believed it to be, i.e. absurdly.

'I've got me own back,' said Brian, clinking glasses. 'Let's drink to revenge. All good writing is revenge, you know that? Joyce, Beckett, Tolstoy. The thing about English writing is, it's soft. No revenge.'

A small, gristly man circled us every so often, like a curious fish at the bottom of a pond. He had facial features astonishingly similar to those of England footballer Stuart Pearce, and the body of a jockey. The fiddle band had struck up on the far side of the bar. Stuart Pearce tripped along in a kind of jig. 'Orlright, Brian?' he said, in a ravaged ninety-a-day voice.

Brian looked up, grinned and waved. Now he was telling me that success would kill you as surely as failure. Brendan had said to him: 'If I hung my balls high enough they'd praise them.'

Stuart Pearce passed round again, and this time he was looking at me. Suddenly he picked up the chair next to me, swung himself into it and poked his nose in my face. 'Have you got a boyfriend?' he asked.

'No,' I said.

'Ever had one?'

'No.'

'Want one?'

'No.'

'Thank God for that. I thought you was a poof!' And Stuart Pearce danced off.

Brian's orbit, and the flying foxes and impertinent dwarves who whizzed round within it, had the skewed hilarity of the stories of Flann O'Brien. Brian told me he was writing a book about a character known as the Sussex Satanist. 'A fatly sexy book.' Derry Mainwaring-Knight, the man who became known as the Sussex Satanist in the course of one of this country's strangest criminal trials, had moved to a posh little village called Newick, north of Lewes, whose inhabitants had more money than sense.

First of all Mainwaring-Knight had befriended the Rector of Newick, the Revd John Baker, claiming he was a Satanist who had been inducted into the black arts by his grandmother, Ethel, when he was eight. A defrocked cardinal had performed the initiation ceremony and shortly afterwards Derry had seen an apparition of Pinocchio standing at the foot of his bed. Pinocchio had told him that from then on his life would be dedicated to destruction. Ethel had arranged for a hole to be drilled in the front of her grandson's head. Two aluminium plates were inserted in his skull which enabled evil messages to be transmitted telepathically, ensuring his complete and helpless slavery to the forces of darkness.

Pouring out this tale to the vicar in a succession of meetings, Mainwaring-Knight had hammed it up by blabbering in tongues, falling into a trance on the night of a full moon, and tearing a Bible to bits. He told the vicar he now wished to escape the clutches of Satanism and lead a blameless Christian life. But to do so he had to destroy the satanic circle to which he belonged, and to do that he needed to obtain the regalia with which his fellow-devil worshippers performed their ceremonies and from which they derived their evil and terrifying powers. The snag was that this regalia, which included Satan's throne, in an office suite off Pall Mall, and the trappings of a temple in an old air-raid shelter in Essex, would cost a great deal of money.

191

The prosecuting counsel in Mainwaring-Knight's eventual trial at Maidstone Crown Court described the Revd John Baker diplomatically as 'charming but gullible'. Brian showed me pictures of him in newspaper reports of the trial which showed him sitting uneasily behind a drum kit in his vestments, and producing a white rabbit from a top hat. Moved by Mainwaring-Knight's sad story, the Revd Baker agreed to ask wealthy and devout Christians living locally if they would care to contribute to a fund he would set up on Mainwaring-Knight's behalf to fight Satanism. Amazingly, several did.

Mrs Susan Sainsbury, wife of the then MP for Hove, gave a few pence short of £80,000; a farmer gave nearly £60,000, a charity worker more than £40,000; a Viscount contributed a white Rolls-Royce Camargue, which cost £37,500, and added a car phone for another £2,500 when Mainwaring-Knight complained that his home telephone was being tapped by Satanists (he consecrated the Roller with 'the ugliest old whore in town', according to Brian); and an Earl handed over £1,000 before becoming suspicious and tipping off the Bishop of Chichester.

Mainwaring-Knight, cosily installed in an attic room in the Newick Rectory, had a rare old time on the proceeds of all this Christian good will. He chanced his way into East Grinstead Theatre during rehearsals for *Peter Pan*, chatted up a pantomime dancer and put her up in a posh hotel for three weeks, paying regular visits for payment in kind. He picked up a prostitute in Southend, bought her a fox-fur coat and rented a bungalow for her, which he also visited frequently. He hired Cadillacs, Lotuses and Range Rovers and passed himself off as a road manager for Pink Floyd and other rock groups. Though he was unable to produce any of the regalia he was supposed to have been buying with all these cash gifts, the Revd Baker was apparently not suspicious, accepting Mainwaring-Knight's explanation that the world of Satanism was necessarily a secretive one, and the less the rector knew the safer it would be for all concerned.

Even after he was arrested on charges of deception, his chutzpah did not desert him. Mainwaring-Knight told the court his money had come from a business he had set up which involved turning prostitutes back into virgins. The girls would be admitted to a private clinic where they received stitches 'in certain places' to restore their hymens. He then supplied these freshly minted maidens to rich overseas clients prepared to pay a premium for them. He had been clearing some £12,000 a week from this enterprise, which accounted for his extravagant lifestyle. The Revd Baker and Peter Ball, Bishop of Lewes, continued to back Mainwaring-Knight through the trial. Wearing a monk's habit in court, the Right Revd Ball spoke of satanic orgies in fields surrounding the Long Man of Wilmington.

The jury found Mainwaring-Knight guilty of fraud and he was sent down for nine years. The seriousness of his offences, according to Judge Neil Denison QC, 'lies not in the enormous sums of money you extracted, but the cynical manipulation of the Christian beliefs of so many good people'. This was what got Brian – that Mainwaring-Knight had been victimized for making a monkey out of the English Establishment, its peers of the realm and its grisly old C of E. He was tickled by the aluminium plates Mainwaring-Knight claimed had been implanted in his head to receive telepathic messages. These were a detail too far, ludicrous on anyone's accounting, especially as he had not, apparently, a touch of scarring anywhere on his balding head. 'Can you—? Can you—?' Brian was laughing too much to get the words out. He reached towards the ceiling to indicate the flow of messages and rapped the front of his own solid, tuberous nut, 'imagine it?'

To swallow Mainwaring-Knight's blatant con trick so completely you had to be fucking stupid. Was it his fault that when he moved to the village of Newick he happened to stumble on a strain of clerical and aristocratic dimness so astounding as to be scarcely creditable? If you or I or anyone took a crazy punt with a complete stranger and said, 'Excuse me, please give me lots of money,' and that person obliged, what would you do? A man had only so much self-discipline. Poor old Mainwaring-Knight had been punished for the stupidity of other people: upper-class, church-going, *English* people.

He had also been punished for exposing a truth about England that the English didn't want to get about: that England was insane; the opposite of what we are taught. England (Brian and I decided between ourselves and the lager and bitter we were putting away) was corralled by a fence of fine mesh ('Fine *mess*?' '*Mesh, mesh*') to keep us from this knowledge. Cleverly built, almost invisible, but a fence nevertheless. You could cut the mesh and go for a walk on the other side, but beware the thought police, the *culture* police, the *class* police (remember, we *were* drunk) who would come and escort you back in the end. Or you could go somewhere where there weren't any fences, like London, where constraints dissolved like ice cubes in hot water, or like Brighton.

Brighton was England with its madness hanging out. The flying fox was proof of this, as was the Sussex Satanist. Everybody had examples of Brightonian madness, which was similar to the buckled logic of the Irish variety. There had been the knickers I had seen on the pavement outside the railway station, looking neatly and freshly stepped out of; round the corner, in the Northern Star pub, a man had been blowing on the bagpipes as if continued planetary existence depended upon it. A friend remembered coming to Brighton during a plague of ladybirds. The ladybirds drifted like red snow in doorways. People scooped them up in handfuls, as they would never pick up other bugs, and tried to dance round them on tiptoe as they walked the pavements. Brian said there was a man on the nudist beach with a long penis he could make rotate madly like a Catherine wheel. He put on a show for tourists. Brian jiggled his head and rolled his eyes.

Stuart Pearce appeared again and circled in diminishing diameters until he slumped down in the seat next to me. 'Sorry

194

'bout that earlier,' he said. 'Nuffin' wrong with gays – 'cept they're poofs!' He roared at his own joke. 'Only issa waste, innit? 'Cos Brighton women, know what I mean? Brighton women, women in Brighton are—' He made big eyes and licked his lips. 'Know what I mean? Big ones, thin ones, fat ones, small ones. I've got all their juices going. Haven't I, Brian?'

A colleague, Bryn Williams, had already told me about the man on the nudist beach with the versatile genitals. Bryn had been doing a story on Roedean School. He had borrowed a bicycle to ride up there, and after freewheeling down the hill on his way back had decided to take a breather on the beach, not realizing it was the nudist area. There – and his Welsh lilt became incredulous, telling the story – he had seen the strangest thing ever, a sort of Brightonian *Déjeuner sur l'Herbe*. There were two male–female couples, obviously friends, sitting on the pebbles passing the time of day together. One couple was fully and rather formally clothed, as if they worked in a solicitor's office and had just popped out in their lunch hour. The other couple wore the briefest of briefs, the woman being topless. Presently, however, the man stood up and peeled off his trunks, and sat down again. Two minutes later the woman did likewise.

All the time the conversation flowed, the smiles and nods and earnest expressions, as if nothing untoward had happened. While Bryn was digesting all this, and deciding it really was one of the oddest little human enactments he had ever witnessed, the man with the rotating penis strolled past, hands on hips, whistling 'Old Man River'.

It was Bryn, in the same conversation, who told me about Francis Carr. Francis Carr was a man who had dedicated the past forty years of his life to proving that Shakespeare did not write the plays attributed to him. From his base somewhere in Brighton, he fired off fortnightly newsletters at academics, journalists and opinion formers, purporting to show that Bacon, not Shakespeare, was the author of the plays, sonnets and long poems. Over the years, Bryn had written several stories on this maddening, endearing eccentric. Bryn knew nothing of the portrait of Guil Shakspeare when he told me about Carr.

Over the summer weeks, with the academic avenues of corroboration seemingly exhausted, Roger had been continuing his psychic investigations into the portrait. After the disappointing meeting at Flo's, and being sent off with a flea in his ear by Derek Nimmo, he decided to try another psychometrist, a psychic gifted in gleaning information from objects simply by handling them. I was out of Brighton at the time. Roger called me afterwards in a state of excitement to tell me what had happened.

Bev, whom he described as 'a short, round woman with corkscrewed red hair who was just about to drop a kid', passed her hand over the picture a few times and then said it was definitely of Shakespeare. She thought the original had been drawn from life by Shakespeare's lover, who was a young man in his acting company. She described this man as small and blond with a foreign accent, probably Dutch. He was not an actor, but probably something to do with feet – a bootmaker, or even a foot massager. He had died young, and Shakespeare had a nickname for him: Balthasar.

This was what had got Roger excited. Balthasar meant nothing to him at the time, but afterwards he discovered that the name appeared in four of Shakespeare's early plays: *The Comedy of Errors* (a merchant), *Romeo and Juliet* (Romeo's man), *The Merchant of Venice* (one of Portia's servants) and *Much Ado About Nothing* (a ballad singer). The last of these, *Much Ado*, was probably written in 1598–9, shortly after the date on the print. The name Balthasar does not appear again in the plays. It was clear to Roger: Shakespeare had been writing small parts for his lover, 'same as Paul McCartney did for Linda in Wings when she came on and played the triangle or the electric toothbrush or whatever. Bev said Balthasar died young. Must have been in 1599, after *Much Ado*, 'cos his name doesn't appear again.'

It made exciting sense. But Roger skated over what Bev said next. He had asked her if she knew the whereabouts of the original portrait from which the print had been copied. She had thought for a moment and then said it was hanging on a wall of a large old house just outside Cardiff. She was unable to be more specific on the location of this house or to give the name of the people who lived there. This information plainly disappointed Roger, though he wouldn't quite admit as much. I understood how he felt. Cardiff was just too prosaic. In this parallel world we had been invited to believe in, anything was possible and the exotic was commonplace, if not practically compulsory. In their past lives people had never been half-wits in Worthing. They had been princesses in ancient Egypt or warriors in the army of Alexander the Great. If we were going on a wild-goose chase, let's at least choose somewhere more exciting than Cardiff! So we neither of us mentioned Cardiff again.

Roger liked the Balthasar angle, though. Through Flo he set up a session with another clairvoyant, unknown to Bev, to see if he could get the readings to match, or at least find common ground. This time I was in Brighton so I went along. Margaret Blunt, who died a few weeks after our visit, had written books and appeared on daytime television. White-haired, given to puzzling but endearing malapropisms, she was as near as the psychic world got to an acceptable public face. She had helped police in murder inquiries, and hit the front pages of the tabloids some ten years ago when an actress in a television soap opera enlisted her help in trying to trace her biological mother. (I remembered the story, but not the outcome – had the actress found her mother in the end? When I asked Margaret, she muttered something about it being a matter of 'material instinct' and 'secret yawnings' and left it at that, from which I understood that the mother had not been traced.)

Margaret lived in a small terraced house in a nondescript part of town near Preston Circus. Sometimes, however smart the appearance they put on for the world, old people can't help letting themselves go in the privacy of their homes. Their eyesight is too weak to see the dust and debris, their arm too feeble to clean the sink. Like them, their houses drift down. The inside of a house is a measure of its owner's morale. By this test Margaret was low. A smell came from the budgie cage, the teacups were stained with tannin, the custard creams were soft. The day's watery sun lit up milky swirls of grime on the windows, and the rat catcher had left a tray of turquoise poison pellets in one corner. 'Nice house,' said Roger, for something to say.

'I find it congenital,' said Margaret. 'Very congenital. Since Jack passed over, I've got my budgie.' Her fingers trembled so much that tea slopped from the cup when she lifted it to her lips. 'You're never alone with a budgie.'

Just when we thought we had made a mistake, and were swapping looks indicating the urgent need to escape, Margaret dispensed with the proprieties and snapped to: pushed her cup aside, leaned forward, put her cards on the table. 'Now,' she said, 'I always warn people first time. It can be a bit alarming. I go into a trance and wait for my spirit guides to pick me up. It'll probably be one of two: the son of Rudolf Steiner, or a Chinese guide called Chang Li. Just so you know, when the time comes, you don't have to call the doctor out!' She smiled, showing ill-fitting teeth. 'Now, I think you have something for me.' Flo had explained to Margaret on the phone that we sought a reading of a portrait of Shakespeare. Roger handed over the portrait. She studied it in her lap, cocking her head on one side. 'A few weeks ago, I was used as a channel by Francis Bacon,' she said, 'who I believe was a cohabitee of Shakespeare.'

'Contemporary.' Roger coughed.

'Mr Bacon told me something interesting would be coming my way. I think he was right, don't you? Now then . . .' Margaret closed her eyes and sat back in her chair. I assumed this was the trance, but it was just a preliminary toe-dipping exercise into the spirit world. She opened her eyes again and said: 'I'm seeing a garden. In France I think. I see bars of shadow on the ground.' She said that to make more sense of this image she would have to go into the trance and trust her spirit guides to come to her aid. 'Remember,' she said, 'don't be alarmed. And don't be afraid to ask questions.'

Margaret sat back deep in her chair, closed her eyes again and took several deep breaths. Then she sat forward and, still with her eyes closed, said 'Welcome' in a ridiculous high-pitched voice. We nodded and then, realizing she had her eyes closed, muttered, 'Welcome' and 'Hello' in embarrassed undertones. This was a joke! Margaret sounded like an extra in a very bad horror film. You expected flimsy scenery to move as she spoke. I dared not look at Roger for fear of exploding in laughter.

Roger was a better sport than me. 'Who are you?' he asked in hollow, sepulchral tones. I hung my head.

'I. Am. Chang. Li,' said Margaret in a cod-oriental accent. 'Chinese sage and spiritual teacher.'

'Welcome, Chang Li,' said Roger. 'What can you tell us about this picture of William Shakespeare. *Is* it William Shakespeare?'

Despite myself I grew interested in what followed. Still talking in her Chinkie-takeaway accent, Margaret said that the portrait was certainly of Shakespeare. The original sketch had been done in colour in the grounds of a building that was part of a church or cathedral. Shakespeare had sat for several drawings in this grassy spot, which was still there and which tourists walked around, though they were not actually allowed on the grass. The place was abroad, but not too far away. On a rock, by the sea.

'What is it called, this place?' Roger asked. 'Where is it?'

Chang Li concentrated hard, but she could not say beyond: 'Velly big, velly tall.'

Then I realized where she meant. Five years before, a Belgian history student had shown us round, attempted to explain in words that weren't his first language the mystical geometry of the cloisters there. This student guide wore a long black coat and round specs and had floppy hair, making him look like an existentialist. His favourite English phrase was 'not at all', which he pronounced 'note a tull'. He worked the phrase into his commentary as often as he could: 'Were ze mernks of Mont St Michel serious fellows? Note a tull.'

Margaret was talking about the ecclesiastical complex of Mont St Michel in Normandy. According to her spirit guide, the original picture, which was later copied to make Roger's print, was still there somewhere, perhaps in a forgotten chamber or tunnel which ran under the grass. The reason the portrait had come into Roger's possession was that Shakespeare now wished it to come to light to put an end to the twentieth-century bickering about what he did or didn't look like. He had chosen Roger to do this because in a previous life Roger had been Shakespeare's uncle. It was Roger, in fact, who had first encouraged Shakespeare's interest in writing. (Even Roger smiled and hung his head at this point.) Roger and I were told by Chang Li to go and find the original picture in Mont St Michel.

It was a bravura performance from Margaret. When she had finished and slumped back in her chair, Roger and I shrugged at each other, thinking the same thing: Mont St Michel was better than Cardiff. Mont St Michel held out possibilities, not least of escape.

I found Francis Carr, the scourge of Shakespeare, in the Brighton phone book. As Bryn had asked rhetorically in one of his articles, 'What has William Shakespeare, late of Stratford-upon-Avon, done to Mr Francis Carr of Brighton?' Carr reserved for Ben Jonson's Swan of Avon the kind of resentment and loathing you might feel towards a bloke who had taken your wife and job, and stamped on your specs for good measure. From what I had read and heard he was obviously an obsessive and probably a crashing bore. But I wanted to find him to show him the Guil Shakspeare portrait and, generally, to hear his side of things. He was charming on the telephone. I caught a stopping train from London to see him in his flat near Preston Park Station.

Francis Carr nurtured a fantasy. One day he would receive a summons from an Establishment figure, a government front-bencher or the editor of *The Times* perhaps. They would arrange to meet in a club in Pall Mall or St James's and over port, surrounded by leather spines, breathing hushed, respectful air, this Important Person would say, 'How about it, Carr, old chap? What on earth are we to do about this Shakespeare business?' Francis admitted it was unlikely to happen. We were talking in his 'office', actually a box room in his small flat. From here he fired off angry missiles of dissension aimed at exploding the myth of Shakespeare's authorship of the thirty-seven plays, 150 sonnets and five long poems attributed to him, and proving that Francis Bacon wrote them instead.

He had other bees in his bonnet: that Bacon also wrote Cervantes' *Don Quixote* and that Mozart was murdered. His head swam with arcane suppositions and deductions which he had assembled into teetering, indignant edifices of 'evidence'. I had assumed that his office, the nerve centre of the one-man war he waged on the world of cosy, thoughtless assumption, would be as jumbled and chaotic as the newsletters which carried his theories to this world. But here, in the eye of the storm, and in contrast to the squalor with which Margaret Blunt surrounded herself, all was serenity and orderliness.

The coffee cups were bone china, sparkling clean. The biscuits snapped. There were three modest bookshelves high up on the wall, with a postcard of the Long Man of Wilmington propped on the lowest. An elderly relative might lodge here, opening her folding alarm clock on the edge of the desk, adding a Georgette Heyer and a velvet-backed hairbrush to the bookshelves, and never feel intimidated by the weight of obsession. Francis Carr might be obsessive on certain questions, but he could also keep proportion. He observed proprieties and laughed at himself. He was modest, not at all a crashing bore but a suburban rebel with a cosmic cause. 'Shakespeare', he said, 'is like an endangered species. The Establishment is rallying round to protect him. But his days are numbered.'

People did not want to hear what Francis had to say. Shakespeare was a building block of our culture but it was rotten, hollow. He wanted to remove the block marked SHAKESPEARE, throw it away and replace it with a solid variety called BACON. But, fearing the culture-wall would fall down, people wouldn't hear of it. So they ridiculed his arguments, but each time they did, patiently, he re-presented them for scrutiny: shake them, stamp on them, hold them to the light, see how solid they are!

For forty years he had been doing this. Of course it did make sense that Bacon really wrote the plays, that Shakespeare, who couldn't spell his own name the same way twice, was, like Frank Windsor, just a jobbing actor. No doubt for big inducements, and who could blame him? he had agreed to be Bacon's front man, his face on history and the world. The theory was well rehearsed. But I wanted the gelignite of batty, obsessional myth-exploding, and Francis tossed me a fine stick, a favourite weapon of Baconians. The so-called nonsense word in *Love's Labours Lost* (spoken by Costard in Act IV Scene 3), '*honorificabilitudinitatibus*', is a Latin anagram: '*hi ludi F. Bacon nati tuiti orbi*'. This translates as 'These plays born of F. Bacon are preserved for the world.' Ha! Stick that in your pipe and blow your head off!

In the 1960s, as the quatercentenary of Shakespeare's birth approached, Francis fronted a campaign to have the Shakespeare tomb and monument in Stratford opened up – a plan denounced by good old Larry Olivier as a 'clodhopping, jack-booted outrage'. Just in time state and Church rallied to frustrate the plan. But, in 1986, they could do nothing to hush up the discovery of a medieval mural in the White Hart Hotel in St Albans. If Francis had been flagging in his life's mission, this was like an amphetamine pill hidden in an orange slice and slipped to a tiring footballer.

This faded wall painting, which showed a young man dying after being gored by a boar, was an illustration of the Shakespeare poem *'Venus and Adonis'*. Experts dated it as no later than 1600 (the poem having been published in 1592 or 1593), which makes the mural the only known contemporary illustration of a work by Shakespeare. But that wasn't the half of it. What got Francis Carr singing to the sky as he walked along was that the White Hart in St Albans was only two miles away from Francis Bacon's country seat at Gorhambury. The White Hart would have been Bacon's local, as it were. Being set apart from the main part of the hotel, was the room containing the mural used by Bacon for secret meetings, perhaps of the Rosicrucian sect of which he was then the leader in England? (And so on . . .)

I judged now as good a time as any to produce Roger's portrait of Guil Shakspeare for Francis to comment on. Francis Carr didn't *really* hate Shakespeare, of course, just the people who stuck blindly with him. Perhaps we did have an authentic likeness of Shakespeare, but would that signify very much if it was merely of a jobbing Elizabethan actor? Francis was fond of analogies. On the phone, when I had told him about the portrait, he had said, 'Ah, but I could show you a fuzzy photograph of a blonde jumping into a swimming pool and say, "That's Marilyn Monroe", and you couldn't prove it wasn't, even if it was really Marilyn Bloggs.'

Now, as I drew a print of the portrait from its cardboard envelope and handed it over, I was expecting him to snort derisively. But he didn't. He had seen many bogus likenesses of Shakespeare, but this was new to him. And the spelling of the name, Guil Shakfpeare, was intriguing. 'Do you think it's possible? . . .' I began.

'"It's possible" . . . is a very big phrase,' he said, and shrugged. It was a dismissive shrug, meaning: What's the point, as it can never be proved either way? But this was precisely the engine that had driven Francis on, the hope that proof might come along. The discovery of the mural in a St Albans pub had been like that. Perhaps Roger and I could discover our own image in a monastery in France.

Francis and I walked slowly through old Preston, the Georgian brick-and-flint villas still looking shocked to be corseted by traffic and fumes after a century or more in deepest countryside. In a pub on the London Road we ordered beef pie and tuna sandwiches and sat in a room with a video game in the corner and a table of lads drinking foreign lager from the bottle. 'People don't like it when you spot that the emperor's got no clothes,' Francis said. And here was another analogy for his life's mission to debunk Shakespeare: it was like walking into a church and shouting, 'Stop this! It's all nonsense.' He would expect to be thrown out, or, at the very least, for the congregation to dispute what he was saying. What he hadn't bargained for was that nobody would even look up. Never mind. He would just shout louder.

One of the lads decided to have a go on the video game, which was called Roadworks. This game, which consisted of steering a mechanical digger over a series of obstacles, made conversation impossible. Each time the digger hit an obstacle the machine juddered, sending vibrations through the floor and up through the soles of our shoes, and made a noise like a freight train passing through the room upstairs (at first I thought it *was* a train, as the pub was near the London–Brighton main line).

We grimaced and waited for the game to be over, and I

had a thought. The reason that Francis's metaphoric church congregation did not respond to his bawlings and bangings-on was that they had crept out of the side door long ago. They were in pubs playing Roadworks and didn't give a monkey's about that old playwright tosser.

Chapter Twelve

It was a weekday morning in early October and my time in Brighton was coming to an end. When I turned into Little Western Street I was half hoping to see someone I knew through the open door of the Grosvenor. I had an errand to run, but I was thirsty too. Half an excuse and I would have been straight in. But I was shocked to find the door closed against the cold wind. All spring and summer that door had remained open and beckoning. By the Grosvenor's unimpeachable reckoning, the Indian summer, a glorious one this year, was over. The beach had been handed back to its metal-detector-heads. The low autumn tides revealed steep shelves of sand at the waterline. Fredda had had a full house for the Labour Party conference – she said a man from the Fabian Society had left a copy of *Hello!* in his waste-paper basket. Now the conference was over, the crowds had gone, and Brighton seemed empty.

Summer in Brighton could be a fool's paradise. You were tempted to put all plans on hold against the glorious light and heat. Real life, messy and sapping, was banished from Brighton. And this was fantastic, a gift of the place, but Brighton, even Brighton, could not destroy real life and so, come autumn, real life was apt to ambush you, pin you down and whisper in your ear: 'What about money? The future? You can't live on light and air, dreams and alcohol, indefinitely.'

When Fredda wasn't on the beach, she had been in a deckchair on her balcony. The floral-patterned deckchair was a fixture there, folded up behind the black wrought-ironwork. But Fredda had sunned her last, this year, and the deckchair had been brought in and returned to the little toilet under the stairs. Perhaps it happened every year at this time: Fredda was having a bit of an identity crisis. Was she an actress or a land-lady? An artiste or an artisan? How could you be an actress if you didn't act? For how long, after you had last acted, were you entitled to call yourself an actress? Fredda needed acting work to remind herself of who she was, preferably a lucrative but easy commercial to ease herself back in. She had a new mugshot done for *Spotlight*, and she worked the phone – pacing the kitchen, glass of wine in one hand, Marlboro Light in the other – for days on end, earbashing producers, agents and old friends to the effect that she was ready, willing and able, while the parakeets squawked, 'She is! She is!' in the background.

But what kind of part could she do? This was the story of Fredda's life. She had studied medical science at Glasgow University, leaving before her final year when she was offered a part in a play at the Edinburgh Festival. If that offer hadn't come along perhaps now she would be a doctor or research scientist. All she asked was to be taken seriously, but, even now, all you saw was a skimpy white uniform – the sexy sitcom medic, all breasts and stethoscope, the bimbo boffin with horn-rimmed specs and horny underwear beneath the lab-coat.

'I went into acting to be a character actress,' she told me defiantly. 'Obviously when I was in *Z Cars* I played a blonde switchboard girl. Then when I was in *Marriage Lines* I was Edward de Souza's girlfriend and of course I had short skirts on and a beehive blond hairdo. When I was in *Steptoe*, the first one, I was the air hostess and I had a little cap on . . . with the blond hair with the beehive and the short skirt. When I was in *Steptoe* again I played the receptionist when he was having his chest X-rayed, but again I had a nice uniform and the short skirt and my . . .' She waved her cigarette above her head, and the smoke bloomed in brief blue semblance of hair. She grinned and shrugged, unsure what to make of it all.

Fredda had recordings of herself on video, which I asked to see. She put them on mid-morning in the ground-floor sitting room. The seafront traffic crossed beyond the net curtains, sounding like waves breaking. Fredda was hoovering the stairs and landings, but kept popping back down, eager to see her thirty-year-old self, see what I thought. In the black and white episode of *Steptoe* she had mentioned, Albert and Harold are summoned for X-rays at a mobile unit. Fredda is the briskly efficient (and all the more sexy for that) nurse behind a desk who takes down their particulars, as it were (this was when viewers learned that the characters' full names were Albert Edward Ladysmith Steptoe and Harold Albert Kitchener Steptoe).

'Any sputum?' she asks, deadpan.

'Pardon?' says Harold.

'Any health problems?'

'I'm as fit as a fiddle – what are you doing tonight?' replies Albert.

As father and son make their way to the X-ray room, Albert says to Harold, 'Tasty piece, isn't she? She's got TB.' Harold looks alarmed. Albert leers in that crumple-jawed, triumphantly disgusting way of his and says: 'Two Beauties!'

'They wouldn't allow that now,' I said, shocked by the crassness.

'But that wasn't *me*,' Fredda said plaintively behind me, gripping a dusty, bulging hoover bag. 'That was me acting the *part* of a dolly-bird.'

A few days later there was a late-night showing on Channel Four of that definitive, iconic sixties film, *Darling*. Fredda appears towards the end in a party scene, in the background, over the shoulder of Laurence Harvey. She wears a little black cocktail dress and is in the middle of a lingering kiss. Presently she and her lover unpeel themselves from each other and go into a bedroom. The light flicks on, then off. The key turns in the lock. In the foreground Julie Christie goes up to Laurence Harvey and says, 'Proceed. Amuse me,' and kisses him. Outside in the street a wretched Dirk Bogarde, Christie's discarded husband, looks up at the lighted window. In this brief sequence was sketched the casual awfulness of which the sixties were capable.

Diana Scott, the character played by Christie in *Darling*, was vapid, selfish and ruthless. It was a misogynistic portrait and a misogynistic trick, to make a young woman stand for the ills of a decade. Fredda wasn't those things, but she did learn, in this woman-hating era, to get her retaliation in first. On one occasion, while engaged to a young television announcer, she went to Greece to shoot a commercial for Craven A cigarettes. She didn't actually smoke in those days, and after fruitless sessions trying to exhale without coughing was fired from the set. On the same day she read in an English newspaper that her fiancé had married someone else. What a way to find out, sitting on a rock a thousand miles away with a throat feeling like hell and a career in embarrassing tatters.

She returned heartbroken, but with a sliver of ice in that heart, also. At a party she picked up a sexy young English actor (a bit of a dolt, by all accounts, though already a household name), took him on to another party at the house of her ex-fiancé and his brand-new wife in Fulham. Did the *Darling* bit, or at least the lingering kiss. Felt better: this was life and how to live it.

These were the kind of parts that Fredda was condemned to, in life as in work, until no one any longer wanted to kiss her lingeringly and lead her off to a bedroom, and the work dried up. Middle age was a drought, in most ways, bar the blessing of children. Now, in the last five years and free of her husband, which was another story, she had found herself eligible for glamorous granny roles, with a tendency towards the zany – she could certainly still play sexy, but elderly sexy

209

was taboo unless you were Joan Collins or Honor Blackman (who looks a lot like Fredda). It was demoralizing, though, turning up for an audition to find a room full of twinsets and K Shoes. *Somebody*'s in the wrong place, she would think, and invariably it was Fredda.

This time round, brown and fit after a summer of sun and swimming, she just knew that the right part, the one commensurate with her experience and wide enough to stretch her, was sitting in a tray in Wardour or Charlotte Street. And when, a week after the new edition of *Spotlight* had come out, and just a couple of days since her hard telephone slog, she got the call, it was the least she expected. In celebration we opened a decent Chablis and she opened another button on her blouse, revealing yet more of the Two Beauties whose bloom had scarcely faded in thirty years.

It was time for me, too, to take stock. I had spent much of the summer in Brighton, returning to London now and then for work and social commitments. The sun, the light, the sense of being on sabbatical from real life, had been overwhelming. Now the book needed wrapping up, life needed to be resumed. And Roger had a plan in that regard.

My errand, when passing the Grosvenor and noting with dismay its closed door, had been to buy a map of Mont St Michel, the mystical monastic site on the Normandy coast where Margaret Blunt had suggested the original of the Guil Shakspeare portrait was hidden. Flo had agreed to ask round a friend and together they would dowse a map of the site to see if they could agree on where the painting might be. They didn't need an elaborate map, she said. One in a guidebook would do. So, reluctantly forgoing a pint in the Grosvenor, I had continued up to the Western Road and bought a copy of the green Michelin guide to Normandy Cotentin, which contained a map and east–west and north–south cross-sections of the mount. Roger's idea was to go to Mont St Michel and, armed with any useful pointers that Flo could provide, try to find the painting. Roger, in fact, was getting carried away. 'Shakespeare trusts me to bring this picture to light,' he said. 'It's a karmic debt he owes me for having encouraged him to write. You coming?'

Flo's friend looked, in respect of her homely ordinariness, like one of the usual psychic suspects. And, like all of the mediums we met in connection with the portrait, bar Derek Nimmo, she desperately wanted to help and would accept no payment. I produced copies of the map and the cross-sections, which I had blown up on a photocopier, and spread them on the coffee table. Roger said we had reason to believe that something – he wouldn't say what – was being kept or hidden somewhere in the place represented by the map.

Dowsing was done with a pendulum of some sort. A thin woman with a fat name, Bessie used an oval of jade on a thin leather strap. First of all she asked the pendulum which direction meant yes. The green stone remained perfectly still for a second or two and then began slowly to move anti-clockwise. This established the lines of communication: if anti-clockwise was yes, clockwise was no; the dowser then proceeded by asking the pendulum a series of questions, as if it were a victim of paralysis with a sole twitching eyelid, or a kidnap victim tapping on a radiator.

Bessie drew the map on to her lap and played the pendulum slowly across it, quartering it methodically. Over the refectory, it twitched. She held it there and said, 'Is something there?' The stone turned anti-clockwise. 'Is it what we are looking for?' The stone turned anti-clockwise again. 'Is it treasure?' The stone twitched, then fell still. Bessie glanced at Roger, who nodded. We marked the point in the refectory with a cross.

We gave Flo the east–west cross section. She had not seen clearly where Bessie had marked her spot, and besides it was impossible, at a glance, to work out where the corresponding spot might be on the cross-section. Using a tiny heart on a chain, Flo hovered near the refectory. She asked a series of questions, moving the pendulum each time, until she was satisfied she had hit the right spot. 'Pen, please,' she said, and marked a cross high up on the eastern wall of a chamber called the Great Pillared Crypt, beneath and slightly to the west of the refectory.

Roger and I developed the plan over several nights in the Grosvenor, huddled at the back away from the main traffic of conversation. First of all, no one else, bar Flo, Bessie and Margaret Blunt, was to know. We would be a laughing stock, he said. People wouldn't understand. I said I wasn't sure that *I* understood. Roger said we didn't have to understand, we just had to do it. We were embarking on a quest, an honourable and time-honoured undertaking, and quests had a habit of turning things up, even if they weren't what you originally had in mind. We liked the idea of the quest and we liked the idea of escape. We toasted both.

A new barman had started recently in the Grosvenor. He brought his own fan club, a couple of whippet-thin boys wearing matching cap-sleeved T-shirts who sat at the bar and gazed at him, barely talking. He was hard-working, aimed to please. During a lull in business he came out from behind the bar with a yellow duster and began to dust the mantelpiece above the electric fire. People stopped and regarded him with amazement. Finally someone said, 'You don't have to do that, love. A lesbian comes in to clean in the mornings.'

It turned out that Fredda knew this new barman. She swanned in one night, subtle in beige and white, vulgar with gold jewellery, and stopped dead in her tracks when she saw him. 'Oh my god,' she said. 'How *embarrassing*. I owe you an apology. And a drink. Let me buy you a drink and I'll explain.'

Fredda's forthcoming audition was for a commercial for a new yoghurt-based dessert and she was excited. A commercial would ease her back in without being too demanding. This one had the added advantage that it would not be shown on British television, so in the event that it was bad she wouldn't have to endure the snide comments that could drive you bonkers after a while. The 'BD to Z Victor One' catchphrase had been the making of her, however briefly; Fredda's equivalent of Larry Grayson's 'Shut that door' or Dick Emery's 'Oooh, you are awful,' and she remembered it with gratitude. But if she really thought back, there had been times when even that had got her down. Complete strangers felt they had the right to march right up to you, holding an imaginary microphone, flicking away imaginary blond locks, and jabber it in your face with pickled onion breath: 'BD to Z Victor *Wun*, BD Z Vic *Wun*, ha ha ha ha B Z V *Wung wung*, come in Z Vic *Wung*, ha ha ha.'

The publicity photographs of her on the walls of the Grosvenor were from this time, this sixties heyday when she had been a public property, however small and trinket-like. One of the pictures showed her wearing the same dress, black with vampish lacy panels, she wore in *Darling*. In it she gazed with something not far short of adoration at the camera. The days were gone when she could adore the lens, but she could still look it in the eye and demand respect, if she got the chance. This audition was about garnering some respect from the lens. It was between her and the camera; the rest of bloody England didn't have to be in on it, and the Scandinavians, French and Spanish would be none the wiser anyway. The product, incidentally, was Swedish PogYog, with chunks of real fruit and a biscuit base.

So, as the audition approached she was getting nervy. What, for instance, should she wear? She was always prepared to go in disguise as a bourgeois matron – the twinset and K Shoes look which she had learned won parts. But in this case the product was Swedish, and the Swedes were a cool, bouncy-breasted lot. She decided to do elegant/sexy,as befitted both her years and her remarkably ageless body. The white, beige and gold look she wore to the pub was a test-run, which I reckoned deserved the thumbs up.

213

For the matron look, she would wear a bra which flattened her chest, removed that straining effect which made her blouse buttons look as if they were about to pop. For the Swedish PogYog commercial, however, she reckoned the straining breasts would be an advantage, so she went up to Marks and Spencer in the Western Road and bought the M&S equivalent of the Wonderbra, an undergarment with impressive powers of lift and separation. But when she got it home and unwrapped it, she discovered that a section of underwiring had come adrift and punctured its silken casing. She pushed it back and tried the bra on, but the wire dug painfully into her sternum.

As she walked back up the hill to the store to return the faulty goods, an idea struck her. Rather than simply swap the bra for one that wasn't faulty, she would make an embarrassing song and dance about it. She would threaten to put the bra on there and then in M&S, she would go so far as unbuttoning her blouse. Acting angry, behaving as an exhibitionist, would be part of getting in the mood for the audition. So this, apparently, was what she did, and the poor chap on the receiving end, behind the customer services counter, had been the new barman in the Grosvenor. 'I'll just call an assistant,' he had said, severely rattled. He pressed a bell. Fredda stood hands on hips with her shirt gaping open, drumming her fingers on the counter-top. A woman supervisor arrived and the young man said, 'We'll just get you a replacement. Er, what size would it be?' He knew it was the wrong thing to say before the words were out of his mouth.

'What size', said Fredda, 'would you suppose?'

Something had been bugging Roger about the Mont St Michel trip – or *quest*, as he insisted on calling it. A quest, said Roger, as we returned to a table out of general earshot at the back of the pub, was a mythical thing. You couldn't take a Stena Line ferry from Newhaven on a *quest*. A lager run to the *supermarché*, yes; quest, no. We discussed options, such as flying to Le Touquet. It still didn't seem right. Then Roger said, 'What about your fisherman friend?'

I had to think. Early summer, when I had gone out with him, seemed a long time ago. 'Jack,' I said eventually. 'Jack was his name.' I remembered him mentioning going to France, how you could be eating frites in no time. In Dieppe, Jack had had frites with mayonnaise and been as sick as a dog for two days. Now he could still eat chips, and he liked mayonnaise in sandwiches and what have you, but chips and frites together? No ways. 'Perhaps if we made it worth his while,' I said doubtfully.

'Imagine it, though,' said Roger, who was on his fourth pint of Harvey's. He framed a picture with his fingers, then turned his hand into a little boat riding the waves. 'Off into the yonder, on a little boat. On a quest for Shakespeare. Have you still got his number?'

I rang Jack the following afternoon, when I gauged he would have returned from the day's fishing. There was a silence while he digested my name, then he said, 'Oh, I remember. Writer feller. 'Noon.' I explained we wanted taking round the Normandy coast, at least as far as Granville if not all the way to Mont St Michel. I did not explain our specific business and he did not enquire beyond asking, 'Legit is it?' I said it was. 'Just a second.' He came back to the phone with a chart, said we'd have to compensate him and his assistant, Wayne, for three days' fishing. The figure he put on this seemed ludicrously low. We fixed a morning and a place to meet.

The day we had fixed was also the day of Fredda's audition. I rose before five, looked from my attic window as I always did before doing anything else, even peeing. This was one's take on the day to come, a way of setting the emotional thermostat. The sky over the ocean was still starry. Not a soul moved on the seafront. It was that brief wedge of time between the respective activities of night and day that was like a little death.

Moonlight shone on the surf, as Graham Greene had once remarked.

Downstairs, I forced down a bowl of cereal. On the kitchen table was an empty bottle of wine and a half-empty pack of Marlboro Lights, the butts in the ashtray bearing smudges of Fredda's lipstick. When I came in the night before, after a quick couple in the Grosvenor with Roger to finalize arrangements, I had seen her sitting there on her own, but decided against joining her. I needed an early night for an early start and, somehow, I needed to be on my own for my last night. We had already settled up the rent bill. Whatever happened in Mont St Michel, when I returned to England it would be to London, not Brighton. I left the house keys on the table, and – on an impulse, thinking French thoughts – scribbled Fredda a note to go with them: *Bonne chance.*

The peace statue had a sheen of dew on her that could have been sweat. What if she, in that wedge of dead night-time when no one was abroad, took wing and flew? Purely for the pleasure of it, like the plane in *Brighton Rock* that advertised something for the health in pale vanishing clouds across the sky. Just a quick turn round the bay. But then, once aloft, you might see the lights of France and realize that Brighton, even Brighton, was still England, and sometimes that wasn't quite enough. One night, perhaps, she would fly too far afield and not return to her pedestal in time. I was suddenly glad to be going to France. Dear old Brighton was a tiring business.

It was cold. I pulled my coat around me. I saw a plume of breath coming round the corner from Little Western Street, followed by Roger. At the same time I heard a spluttering engine and saw, from the other direction, Jack's red van materializing through the gloom. 'Here we go,' said Roger, patting his pockets. 'Got the picture, got the maps, passport, phrasebook . . .' Jack pulled up, leaned across and wound down the passenger-side window. ''Nin,' he said.

''Nin,' we said.

We jammed into the fish-smelling cabin alongside Jack, me with the gearstick digging into my right leg, Roger with his rucksack on his knee, and kangarooed off along the seafront, the fairy lights looking like Vaseline lamps in the fuzzy dawn. Roger fiddled with the side pocket of his rucksack, pulled free his hipflask and offered it around. 'Breakfast, anyone?' he said.

Here is the final reel, no bigger than a side plate.

A twitten ran between high flint walls separating the back gardens of Clifton Terrace and Vine Place. To check up on Nellie, the sister of his late lover, Edward le Bas needed only to walk down his garden in Vine Place, through the gate at the end, cross the twitten and enter Nellie's garden in Clifton Terrace through a corresponding gate. Now Nellie had developed the trembling disease, Edward made a point of looking in every day, though never too early.

Brighton was not a place in which one rose early. Edward generally surfaced at around eleven, soothed his sore head and sluggish limbs with a bath, and paced his attic studio while smoking the first of the day. And as he did so he looked out over the rooftops of Clifton Terrace to the sea, to France and beyond, and in his mind's eye saw light even sharper than Brighton's, saw pop-bright frescoes in Renaissance *chiese*, yearned after the shoulderblades of bare-topped boys in Agadir, tasted oysters and Muscadet in a Normandy port.

Edward dedicated himself to escape. After prep and public school, university and art college, he had been expected to enter the lucrative family steel business. His decision to go his own way angered his father, who initially cut his allowance, though Edward did eventually inherit the family millions. Throughout his life, he fulfilled an obligation to attend the annual shareholders' meeting at Claridges, where he would sign the necessary papers, turn up his collar and head for the bar as swiftly as business allowed. His was a life lived in flight from uptight old England, the ball and chain of Harrow, the shackles of Cambridge, the mausoleum of gentlemen's clubland.

In England he had houses in Bloomsbury and Chelsea, Rye and Brighton, places to let your hair down, on the edge of the respectable, and, in the case of the two Sussex towns, on the edge of England also. But even Brighton wasn't enough of an escape, sometimes, and he just had to jump England's emotional bail and head for Europe. This was why Nellie had his beloved Polly on permanent loan in Clifton Terrace, because he could never stay put in one place for any length of time.

At a dinner party in Wandsworth I met a man called Robin whose artist mother had lived in Clifton Terrace in the 1960s. Would she have any recollection of this chap, Edward le Bas? I wondered. Robin rang his mother, now a very old lady living in St Ives, on my behalf and called me a couple of days later. Of course she remembered Edward, how could one forget him? He had lived round the back of the terrace in Vine Place – was charming, handsome and, most of the time, drunk. He had had a bulldog who attacked Robin's mother's poodle, for which he was cravenly apologetic. He was solicitous of a silver-haired lady called Nellie who looked a bit Japanese and lived next door but one to Robin's mother. Nellie had got a shaking disease. One year for her birthday Edward had bought Nellie a mink hat – splendid enough, to be sure, Nellie had said to Robin's mother, but completely useless, seeing as she never went out of the house these days. Edward should think before he acted, that had always been his trouble.

By eleven-thirty, when Edward walked through the kitchen door of Clifton Terrace and into Nellie's front room, she would just be finishing breakfast. It was a fine room in which to eat breakfast, as fine in its way as those greenhouse appendages of the seafront hotels where residents, like tomatoes, ripened in the sun. Here, rather than the narrow proximity of water, you got the full sweep of downland contours, the infinite glaze of sea disappearing into sky. It was a view of hope and possibility that rarely failed to uplift him, and only then when the rain was so thick it had turned to cloud and you couldn't see to the other side of the road, let alone as far as the Metropole domes and the sea.

This had struck him from the very early days in Brighton. One bright spring morning not long after the war, when Nellie was having breakfast with her housekeeper, Mrs Jones, Edward had turned up with a sketchpad, a box of coloured chalks and a twinkle in his eye. 'Carry on, ladies, don't mind me,' he had said, dragging a chair from the table and placing it against the back wall.

'What are you doing?' asked Nellie, cup poised between saucer and lip. 'You're never drawing us! What a cheek! We do mind, Mrs Jones, don't we?' But Nellie was pleased, of course.

'Not drawing *you*, no, ladies. Good heavens, no. What a presumption! Drawing the window, and the view. And if you happen to get in the way, well I suppose I may be forced to render the august presences of your ethereal forms ... and how are you this fine morning, Nellie? Looking well ...' And so he worked at speed, bantering all the while, telling Mrs Jones she could leave the breakfast things exactly where they were, he would tidy them himself, and *that* would be a turn-up for the books, if she would be so kind as to hold that cup just like that, in mid-air, for a minute more ... until he had knocked off this exercise in light and composition, laid the pad on the edge of the breakfast table and lit up a cigarette. Nellie took the pad, squinted critically at Edward's work.

'Just a quick scribble, Nellie,' he said, exhaling sibilantly.

'But it's so *messy*, Edward,' said Nellie. 'Don't you believe in straight lines?'

Fifteen years on, Edward's routine of visiting Nellie in the mornings had hardened into habit. Now that she was ill, scarcely going out, and the new housekeeper did not live in, she relied on his visits. Now her hands shook as she ate breakfast. The cup rattled in its saucer as she picked it up. The tea spilled down her front as she drank. What was worse, her mind was going shaky, too. She had begun to confuse Edward with his own dog, treat him as if he were of the genus *Canis*. 'Down,' she would instruct sternly when he walked into the room. 'A dog is a quadruped, not a performing flea. Now where is your master, where is Edward?'

For Edward's favourite young relative, a little girl, seeing 'Auntie' Nellie was an ordeal. The little girl came down from a big house in the Sussex countryside to see her Uncle Edward. She loved seeing him, and being taken on the seafront and allowed on the ferris wheel on the pier-end. Edward made her laugh by putting daubs of paint on the end of his nose and pretending to be fast asleep as he walked; he was not like an uncle, more like a same-age friend. But Nellie! Errrgghh! Nellie smelled. Did she *have* to go and see her? Could Edward not pretend to Nellie that she had not come down for the weekend after all? 'But that', said Edward, 'would be fibbing.'

'Only a *little* fib,' said the little girl.

'Sounds like quite a big fib to me,' said Edward. 'Or a medium-sized fib, at least. But I know something better than fibbing.'

'What's that?' said the little girl.

'Funning. Much better than fibbing.'

Edward and the girl crossed the twitten and entered Nellie's house via the garden. Once they were in the kitchen, Edward got down on all fours and signalled silently for the girl to do likewise. Then he reached up, turned the knob and pushed the door into the front room slowly ajar. Edward shuffled forward on all fours and the little girl followed. Nellie was sitting in the wing-backed armchair with the red cushion you can just see in the corner of the painting, eyes closed, mouth open in a semi-doze. As the door creaked and then stopped she opened her eyes and looked puzzled, then alarmed. 'Edward?' she said. 'Is that you?'

'*Ruff.*' From down on the carpet, Edward barked. With his back foot he tapped on the carpet encouragingly, and the little girl barked too.

Nellie looked down and, perfectly lucid for once, opened her eyes wide in amazement. 'Good heavens, Edward! Have you gone completely mad? What's got into you? Get up off the floor at once. And who's that behind you? Is it—? *What* an example to set a little girl.'

Later, back in his studio in Vine Place, Edward poured a stiff Scotch and let the little girl prise out the ice cubes that came from his very fine American refrigerator. 'Now, what we do next really will be fun, I promise,' he said.

'What's that?' she said, pulling a face as she tried to suck an ice cube. 'I didn't like the last fun,' and she shuddered at the memory of a livid 'Auntie' Nellie.

'See that chair?' He pointed at an old wooden, paint-spattered chair, walked over and hoisted it between two fingers, drinking his Scotch with the other hand. 'Ahhhh.' He swallowed, swung the chair in front of the window facing the sea and positioned it there. 'I'm going to paint a picture of it.'

'The chair? That's not very fun.'

'Ah, but here's the interesting bit. I'm going to paint a picture of the chair *with you sitting in it.*'

The little girl's feet did not quite reach the ground. She sat side-on to the window, so he could get her profile and she could still look out. He got her to gaze out of the window. 'Look far away,' he said. 'At the horizon. Even further.' She was a very good sitter, patient and still, as if the horizon had hypnotized her.